A Video Course book!

The Last Martial Arts Book

Nine Square Diagram Boxing

Al Case

For information concerning books and videos by Al Case, go to:

MonsterMartialArts.com

This is NOT the same Nine Square Diagram Boxing course
that is offered at MonsterMartialArts.com.

Please go to Monster Martial Arts
for advanced studies in this art.

TABLE OF CONTENTS

SPECIAL NOTE

Rarely, a link to a video won't work.

Try typing the link into your browser.
Try a different browser.
Try a different computer.

If no joy you can email me at aganzul@gmail.com.

ANOTHER SPECIAL NOTE

For more information on Nine Square Diagram Boxing go to MonsterMartialArts.com, or to…

https://9squarediagramboxing.wordpress.com

AUTHOR'S NOTE

Some people may wonder at the title. Simply, this book replaces all other martial arts books.

This book, which is to say the Art of Nine Square diagram Boxing, uses the science of matrixing, so everything is logical, and everything fits together. You will, by the time you finish this book, understand how different arts work together.

It has the usefulness of Karate. It is useable on the street or in the ring. The forms and the techniques are directly applicable to the real world.

It has the meditative aspects of such arts as Tai Chi Chuan and Pa Kua Chang. It has the peace of mind and breeds the philosophical outlook, or maybe you want to call it the 'inlook,' of zen.

It has all the techniques of every art, but combined and condensed into simple, easy to learn modules. You will shortly be able to slide from module to module, or technique to technique, or even art to art, as you wish.

This book is the last book you will ever need to do on the martial arts. It includes all arts, condenses all concepts to workability, changes the mind and soul, and, dare I say it…it is fun.

It is fun to finally get the truth, delve into the soul, and become the truly competent person you are.

PREFACE

Guaranteed, in reading this book you are likely to get frustrated. This is because I am asking you, no matter how simple I make it, to think in higher concepts. The mind, of course, shrieks, 'NO!'

To guard against the frustration and aggravation in learning how to think at a higher level let me tell you how it works.

A student of engineering is given a schematic of a house. The teacher points at one little scribble of lines, out of the dozens and dozens of scribbles of lines, and says, this is the pipe leading from the kitchen to the bathroom.

The student scratches his head, gets confused, frustrated, aggravated… much the same as a student of Karate gets when presented with concepts of higher intelligence.

So the instructor tells the engineering student to take his map, and a flashlight, and to crawl under the house.

The student crawls under the house. He is cursing because he bumps his head on the beams, runs into cement blocks, rubs his knees and elbows raw. Furthermore, he can't get the map to stay open, the flashlight is weak and hard to focus, and he doesn't understand the 'landmarks.'

BUT…he finds the pipe and puts his hand on it. He crawls, slowly and painstakingly, and follows that pipe through the darkness. He studies the map, changes the flashlight batteries, and follows that pipe under a maze of rooms. He comes to a place where pipes lead up, and he realizes he is under the kitchen.

OH MY GOD! I have found it. Understanding. Enlightenment. And the student of engineering now can become a full fledged engineer. He has the understanding, you see.

So when you are boggled by a matrix, or the technique doesn't make sense…grab a flashlight and look at your copy of this book and force yourself through the darkness. Don't think about it…DO IT!

In the end, you will slap your head and wonder why you made it so difficult. But, of course, by then you will be capable of higher thought.

Guaranteed, everybody who gives me one star is justifying the fact that they couldn't reach the higher thought.

Everybody else, the five star people, they took their flashlight and followed the directions of this book…to the letter.

Have a great work out!

Al

INTRODUCTION

I began the martial arts in November, the Monday after Thanksgiving, in 1967. At first I thought it was all a joke, but within three lessons I was convinced, and I knew I would be doing the martial arts for the rest of my life.

I began with Chinese Kenpo, studying Rod Martin Chinese American Karate Kung Fu. This was an offshoot of Tracey Brothers and Ed Parker. It was probably the third (of five) kenpo systems that Parker created. I became an instructor, wrote the training manual for the school, and moved on.

Eventually I began studying under Robert J. Babich (Bob) at the Kang Duk Won in San Jose. This was a pure form of Karate, taken from a lineage that did not pass through Japan, and was probably as close to the original karate invented on Okinawa as it was possible to be.

Bob was the finest martial artist I have ever seen. He had studied with Don Buck, the 'Tiger of Benecia,' and Mas Oyama. That art was Kyokushinkai. In an interesting turn of circumstance, Bob began studying Kang Duk Won under Norman Rha, and he would give up Kyokushinkai and make the Kang Duk Won his art.

I received my black belt from Mr. Babich in March of 1974, and shortly after that he retired.

For the next twenty years I bounced around, meeting people, studying various arts, and learning as much as I could. I spent a lot of time comparing and taking apart various systems, and combining them into more logical form. This would be the start of matrixing, and the actual technical path I followed is outlined in five books I wrote detailing the systems I was going through and making into something else.
Following are the five books that are an accurate record, in form and technique, of how I came to understand and master Karate.

Pan Gai Noon (Half hard/half soft ~ Chinese Kung Fu) a research into the roots of one of the Okinawan Karate systems.

Kang Duk Won (House for Espousing Virtue ~ Korean Karate) Probably the most pure version of Karate, as envisioned by the men who created it.

Kwon Bup (Fist Method ~ American Karate) A purely America form of Karate inspired by the Kang Duk Won.

Outlaw Karate ~ Two arts (KDW and KB) broken down to their most useful techniques and made into one art.

Buddha Crane Karate ~ The last attempt to make sense of Karate before Matrixing was properly formed.

I studied many other arts past karate, including but not limited to:

Wing Chun
Tai Chi Chuan
Pa Kua Chang
Southern Shaolin
Northern Shaolin
Aikido
Various Weapons

Each of these arts contributed to my store of knowledge, acquainting me with such concepts as fixed position flow, moving position flow, various types of grab arts, harmony in motion, and so on.

If one truly masters Karate one can easily master the arts beyond Karate, and which will educate a person in concepts beyond karate and inherent in the whole martial arts.

The problem, of course, is that there are very few examples of real karate these days, and no instructors of the caliber of Mr. Babich.

One can master the martial arts, but one would pretty much have to duplicate the path of writing and studying and analysis that I have done.

Better to just learn matrixing, avoid the false conclusions, and move to the top of the mountain.

What I have done is fairly evident in the books and videos I leave behind. These materials provide a pathway that will enable any person to master the whole martial arts. Not just an art or two, but all of them.

In the early 1980s I began writing for the martial arts magazines. I would eventually write some 30+ articles. I also had my own column, 'Case Histories,' for four years.

During this time I opened a series of schools. I taught everywhere, on rooftops, in basements, in alleys. I had my own dojos, and I went through a variety of arts, searching for the best method for teaching the martial arts. This proved to be a very satisfying period of time, and I learned much, and learned that I had much to learn.

Now I am closing in on old age. I will be 72 by the time I am finished writing this tome. And what is the subject of this little epistle?

My art, my conclusions after over 50 years researching and developing the martial arts.

My art is founded in Tai Chi, but draws from a variety of concepts which demonstrate, and teach, the whole martial arts.

You will be able to go slow, as in Tai Chi, but pulse your punch, as in good Karate. The teaching modules are simple and logical. There is a direct correlation between form and applications, and it is all applicable to freestyle.

You will find the best parts of many arts here, and the corrected concepts of other arts.

The concept of Nine Square Diagram Boxing, which is what I call this art, is simple, yet profound. The Art takes into account all angles of attack and defense, and in a more comprehensive and logical format than any art that has come before. All techniques can be matrixed, which is to say linked one technique to another, one art to another.

Having said all that, I must insist on one profound fact: The whole art is based on…Basics.

I have said it before, and I will always say it: *there are no advanced techniques, there are only better basics.*

Thus, the format includes a series of simple techniques done on a nine square diagram. The techniques are repeated endlessly, yet in their simplicity they contain all the moves of the martial arts.

Further, done properly, the exercise will strengthen the body and mind as no other art does.

And, a caution here: do the art, module by module, taking your time. It may seem silly to just do the same move on a nine square diagram, but it provides a context of meditation that will expand your art endlessly.

To do a random form, a bunch of unrelated sequences, for a few months and think you have learned a something is silly. To do one of the nine square forms for a few months, so simple, will cement a basic understanding in you that cannot be refuted.

The freestyle portion of this art is similarly simple…yet profound. It is based upon growing the actual awareness of the individual, enabling them to properly utilize the nine movements as they become able to 'think within the moment.'

To be clear, however, it is not 'thinking' that is actually done, but rather the development of intuition.

So this is my history, how I trained in both martial arts and writing, and how I ended up with this art, Nine Square Diagram Boxing.

Is there more to be done? Of course. I would love to be vain and say: This art is the best! But my own experiences over more than 50 years have easily proved that no art is superior, that the true art is a living, growing thing.

The only only thing to remember, when making this art your own, is that the true art must align with the simplest concepts possible.

Thus, don't add, rather grow your database, then ruthlessly trim it down.

In conclusion let me say one thing.

When I began writing, over 50 years ago, and began martial arts at almost the same time, I had one thought in my mind. I remember it clearly even now, as clear as the day I had it.

I wanted to write books that would be a letter that people would read in a thousand years.

I want people to get the same enlightenment and joy out of studying the martial arts that I have.

Thus, while some would say that the sheer volume of work I have done, augmented by the millions of words I have written, is too much…I offer this book.

This is my art. This is what I do, and it will last a 1000 years. And more.

If you are truly dedicated, you will search out my other books and writings and videos. If you see how I did what I did then what you do will be that much more powerful.

Have a great work out!

Al Case

Chapter One
Basic-Basics

Most martial artists think the art is basics. Well, yes, but they often miss the true underlying foundation behind all basics, which I call the Basic-Basics.

Basics are the kick and the punch, the various blocks, and the stances.

But these basics, no matter how much practiced, will never work to the fullest unless the artist makes a profound study of the Basic-Basics.

These next couple of pages I will describe the Basic-Basics, and I suggest you study, ponder, dissect, analyze and, most of all, apply to your Basics. *Basic-basics are the secret of the True Art.*

RELAX

It is the truth that when you tighten a muscle energy passes through that muscle, and limb, slower and with less efficiency. Or, to say it another way: Tight muscles stop energy. Or to say it another way: Tight muscles inhibit motion.

Which is to say this: Energy flows best through loose muscles.

The proof of this is simple: tighten your muscles, then punch. Then loosen your muscles and punch. The looser muscle is faster than the tighter muscle.

Thus, you should practice relaxing at all times.

There is a Japanese saying: Stand squarely in the room.

This means that you should stand, posture correct (we will discuss correct posture shortly), and relax so that you can move easily and quickly in the eight directions.

And, once you have done this, you should practice relaxing in every stance and every configuration of arms. You should be able to move in any of the eight directions quickly and easily, without the need to unbalance the self, to 'pre-lean' in any direction prior to moving in a direction.

The final piece to this idea of relaxing is this: Loose-tight.

When I originally learned karate I was told to tighten up the whole body on impact. Fortunately, I moved on from that less than adequate teaching and learned that one should only tighten the fist…atop a correctly structured body. And, beyond that, to not tighten anything at all; to just stick your limb through another body as if thrusting a stick through a watermelon. It was at this point that I learned the secret of striking with 'chi power,' and how much more efficient it was, and how to unleash Intention, which is the most powerful force in the universe.

To conclude this section on Relaxing let me say this: Karate means 'empty hands,' and the empty, in Empty Hands, is in the concept of relaxing. Relax, and you will learn True Karate, and True Martial Arts.

BREATHING

The secret to relaxing, and to other such subjects such as chi generation, grounding the weight, iron fists and blocks, and so on, is best realized through proper breathing habits.

To learn to breath properly stand with the feet shoulder width apart and pointing straight forward.

Inhale air and then exhale it. When you exhale push the sensation of air to the diaphragm, then from the diaphragm to the Tan Tien.

Tan Tien means 'The One Point,' and it is the Japanese name for the main energy center in your body. It is located at a point approximately two inches below your navel and inside your body.
When you inhale again keep your attention on the Tan Tien. Focus on the sensations of the Tan tien, and the muscles surrounding that core of the core.

The sensation of air going down through the lungs to the diaphragm, when it passes through the diaphragm, becomes a sensation of energy.

When the sensation of the energy condenses into the Tan tien, the Tan Tien will create energy. There are several proofs for this.

The first proof is to stand with the feet shoulder width apart, feet pointing forward, and extend your arms and fingers to the sides. If you are relaxed then you will feel, when the air/energy hits your Tan Tien, a tingling sensation in your fingertips.

A second proof would be to stand with correctly with your wrist, palm up, on a partner's shoulder. Your arm should be slightly bent. Make your arm tight and it will be easy for your partner to collapse your arm by pulling down on the inside of the elbow. But if you relax, breath to the Tan Tien and imagine a flow of energy coming from the Tan Tien up through the body and out the arm, it will become unbendable, even for number sof people pulling down on the inside of the elbow.

A third proof would be to simple stand correctly and make a circle of your thumb and forefinger. Have a partner pull the fingers apart, not sideways, but directly apart.

At first the partner will be able to pull your fingers apart easily. But if you simply trace a circle with the finger of your other hand around the circle of the thumb and forefinger, and imagine energy flowing in that circle, your fingers will not be able to be separated, even if you have one people pulling on your thumb and another person pulling on your forefinger.

A final proof (though there are many more ways to prove what I say here), is the Energy formula.

The Energy Formula is:

$$Weight = Work = Energy$$

If you stand with your feet apart you do not work hard, and the Tan Tien creates little energy, just enough to prop yourself up.

If you spread your feet a foot, and slightly bend the legs, you will obviously work harder. Your legs will start to feel the strain, and you will shortly have to breath harder.

Why breath harder? Because that creates more energy which you can use in stance.

If you spread your feet further and assume a deep horse stance your tan tien must create much more energy. Thus, you breath deeply to the Tan Tien. If you focus on your breathing correctly, and steel your mind to the fact that you can do this, and that *any pain you suffer will not kill you,* then shortly you will be able to stand for long lengths of time in the horse stance. Simply, you will have the mental discipline, and the energy.
You will notice, as you go through these proofs, that they do not require muscle to work, only a change of mental attitude.

Practicing these simple proofs, and the stances and forms you will read in this book, you will easily reach a place where nobody can unbalance you, or lift you off the ground.

This all being stated, there are several rules you must follow when breathing.

1. Always breath to and from the Tan Tien.
2. Create a wave of Energy to and from the Tan Tien.
3. Practice flowing energy from the Tan Tien into the body part striking, or being struck.
4. Always strive to breath out when the body expands, and in when the body contracts.

If you have a disagreement with anything I have said here, better read the material again and make sure you understand it, for I have deemed it true after 50 years of research and practice.

GROUNDING

Grounding is when you sink your weight, and it is more than that.

The Chinese often say you must 'root' yourself to the ground. This description is closer to the truth, but not being entirely adequate because it is grounded in mysticism and not physics.

To fully understand the concept of grounding I recommend you look to definitions available in electronics. Hard physics will make mystical descriptions understandable, and you will better understand the concept of grounding.

When you take a stance it is not to make your legs strong, it is to connect you to the surface you are standing on. This is what grounding actually is.

There are actually two purposes to the legs: to move your body, or to hold to the ground.

Kicking is a minor purpose.

Thus, if you practice the drill from the fourth proof, using the Energy Formula, you will learn how to sink your weight into the ground so that you cannot be dislodged. This will give you a good platform from which to launch punches and blocks and even kicks.

If you practice your stances with the idea of one leg being a coiled spring placed in the earth, then you will be capable of covering distances quickly, and thus striking with the weight of the entire body.

If you sink your weight at the same time as you drive your weight into the earth it will be as if you are 'throwing a planet' at the opponent. The more weight you feel in your stance the more weight you will be able to put in your strikes and blocks and kicks.

Interestingly enough, your ability to send energy down the legs is more important than stance training. Stances make your legs strong, but we are looking for the creation of energy, not muscle. Thus, you can do the forms with high stances if you can increase the sensation of weight inside the leg.

ALIGNMENT

Alignment is when the parts of the body support one line of energy, one intention.

Thus, stand in a stance and assume a posture. When your partner pushes on your fist you should feel weight traveling on a line through your body to the ground.

If your body gives way, then find the point which gave way and adjust it.

This is called Body Testing, and *if you do it through all postures and applications you will find the True Art.*

While this idea of alignment, and testing it through Body Testing seems simple, it must be done through every stance, and every configuration of the body. This concept, of testing all possible postures and stances, is a good reason for studying a variety of forms and applications from all arts. If there is any single secret behind why I was able to discover the things I have discovered, it is this concept of Body Testing.

Here are some examples of correct body alignment:

1. Pointing the feet to the front uses the feet the way they are designed. You don't slap the feet down, but rather 'roll' them, using the arch as a spring.
2. The knees should be pointed forward. This idea of aligning feet and knees will go a long way towards eliminating the need for knee or hip replacements as one grows older. Simply, if you have wear on one side of your shoe or the other, this indicates 'pronation,' and there will be resultant 'counter pronation (or 'wear') through the knees or the hips. Check your shoes right now and discover whether you have been using the body the way it has been designed.
3. The shoulders should be over the hips. If your shoulders are in front of the hips you can be pulled off balance. If your shoulders are behind the hips you can be pushed off balance. Either condition will effect the power of your strikes and blocks. As for twisting, you must examine the stance and posture (through body testing) to see if it is feasible.
4. The tan tien should be between the feet. The lower body is a triangle, and the apex of the triangle must not be outside the base, else you will easily be unbalanced, and you can even suffer damage to the body if it is overstressed in such a bad position.
5. Study the triangles of the arms and upper body.

CBM
(COORDINATED BODY MOTION)

CBM is when all parts of the body support one intention...*while in motion.*

It sounds the same as Body Alignment in a certain way, until you add the concept of being in motion.

Simply, each body part must be studied and utilized so that each body part contributes weight in motion appropriate to its percentage of the strike.

This concept can be studied in a variety of forms and in applications. This is another reason to learn a variety of forms, and even arts.

A simple way to begin this study is to simply: *Begin the motion of all body parts at the same moment in time. End the movement of all body parts at the same moment in time.*

Doing this will lead you into the True Art, and it will do so by forcing you to ask certain questions. For instance:

What should the position of a foot in a stance be to create maximum traction, and thus enable maximum push.

Or: how low should the body be to maximize the energy of the stance while not disabling the ability to spring quickly.

Or: which body part should I be breathing into at which time to create 'pulsing' power.

And so on.

The ancient method for expressing this concept of CBM is to 'Use the body as one unit.' A good expression, but lacking in exact description, and therefore results.

Chapter Two
Footwork Diagram

There is a mathematical logic to Diagram Boxing.

You are a point in all directions. (This defines 'awareness,' which is what you are when you take away the body. To fully understand this simply ask yourself who is looking through your eyes. That is 'Awareness.'

Two points make a straight line. Interestingly, while a line is assumed to be the shortest distance between two points, an accomplished Martial Artist knows that a line is not the shortest distance. This may not seem logical, but only to those who have not gone anywhere in the martial arts. Once one has done enough of the martial arts, and has broken loose from the dictates of Newtonism, one will realize that universe is quite malleable, and geometries exist only as parameters designed to contain the human spirit. The parameters of Newtonianism can be bent, or even broken.

Science is a measurement of the universe, but there are things in this universe that cannot be measured. These things are usually dissed, scoffed at as the 'fake' science of the paranormal, and so on.

But that is only science failing to measure something they don't understand. Which is to say there is something outside the limits of Newtonian science. And this something, if measured, would expand the knowledge of man.

Which is to say that there is something larger, a broader science, which is not understood, and which encompasses the smaller science of Newton.

The Martial Arts, when done the correct way, which would include correcting all the structures of the body, through all the methods of the martial arts, which is easily accomplished by studying Matrixing and applying it to your art, lead the individual to this 'science beyond Newton.'

For those of you who do not fully comprehend what I have just said, let me include a short passage from Principia Cybernetica Web.

*The world view underlying traditional **science** may be called "mechanistic" or "**Newtonian**". It is based in reductionism, determinism, materialism, and a reflection-correspondence view of knowledge. Although it is simple, coherent and intuitive, it ignores or denies human agency, values, creativity and evolution.*

Further down the page is more elucidation.

The elements of the Newtonian ontology are matter, the absolute space and time in which that matter moves, and the forces or natural laws that govern movement. No other fundamental categories of being, such as mind, life, organization or purpose, are acknowledged. They are at most to be seen as epiphenomena, as particular arrangements of particles in space and time.

And I am saying that as you pursue the martial arts, as you gain in correct (matrixed) discipline, elements that are not included in the Newtonian Viewpoint, such as certain mental activities, intuition, the human effect on matters of space and time, values (especially virtue based), life, purpose, creativity, and so on, will manifest.

These properties define a whole universe, a universe beyond the Newtonian universe, and which includes the Newtonian universe.

To continue with the mathematical logic of this chapter: Three or more points make a plane.

Planes can make a form.

Forms can make all the structures of life which we think are real, and which we allow to bind us.

Having gone a lot further than I originally intended, let me offer a list (evolution) of shapes, or forms, which are used, or can be used, in Nine Square Diagram Boxing.

LINE WORK ~ One can shuffle, step, pivot, or turn while on a straight line.

CORNER WORK ~ One can move ones foot inside or outside one's other foot, which gives 16 potentials of stepping. One can elaborate further by jumping and twisting on the four corners with both feet simultaneously.

FOUR SQUARE WORK ~ One can set up four boxes in one, the sides to be shoulder width for each box.

NINE SQUARE WORK ~ As defined in this book, there are virtually unlimited possibilities for stepping, especially when joined with arm configurations and potentials for hand work.

CIRCLE WORK ~ Can be used Pa Kua Chang style, or a combination of Nine Square Diagram Boxing and Pa Kua, and in two man and more sets.

Past this one gets into odd geometries that don't always fit together, and make learning random, illogical and difficult. This would be the province of classical forms.

That said, one should not discount the classical forms. Just because matrixing puts logic to the martial arts doesn't mean we throw out the baby with the bathwater and discard the inventions of those who have practiced and handed down the martial arts over the millennium. I am particularly fond of going through the classical forms and searching for odd movements which can be matrixed, restructured in a more logical manner, or just done because they are cool, or work, or whatever.

Chapter Three
The Basic Form

Below are the videos for the nine square basic forms.

9 square diagram low block.mp4
https://youtu.be/xYWL8bjeJmM

9 square diagram high block.mp4
https://youtu.be/0ljTz---CPs

9 square diagram outward block.mp4
https://youtu.be/IzO7jPwl2rM

9 square diagram knife hand.mp4
https://youtu.be/QVPiC35CaBY

9 square rhythmic freestyle.mp4
https://youtu.be/dY7g0lFX-aM

HOUSE ONE

The following two forms are the basic forms. They put the circle of blocks that is karate into two simple but logical forms. They should be done solo, and as two man forms. Below is the Circle of Blocks.

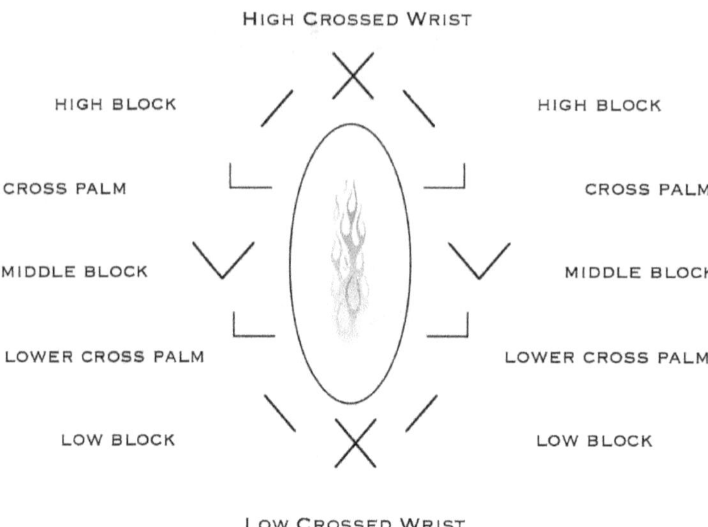

House One presents the low block, high block, outward block and palm block on a back and forth linear pattern.

House Two presents the crossed wrist low block, the crossed wrist high block, the inward block and the double outward inverted blocks.

Examine the graphic above and you will find all blocks represented.

Do the form slowly at first, build up speed only as your partner builds a tolerance for pain.

HOUSE ONE

1   Attacker steps forward with the left foot into a front stance and punches to the belly with the right hand.

Defender steps back with the right foot into a back stance and executes a left low block.

2   Attacker shifts/steps forward into a front stance and executes a right punch to the chest.

3   Attacker steps forward with the right foot into a front stance and punches to the chest with the left hand.

Defender steps back with the right foot into a back stance as he executes a right outward middle block.

4   Defender shifts/steps forward with the right foot into a front stance and executes a left punch to the chest.

5   Attacker steps forward with the left foot into a front stance as he executes a right punch to the face.

Defender steps back with the right foot into a back stance as he executes a left high block.

6   Defender shifts/steps forward with the left foot into a front stance and executes a right punch to the chest.

7   Defender becomes the attacker and steps forward with the left foot and strikes to the belly with the right hand.

Attacker becomes defender and steps back with the right foot into a back stance as he executes a left downward block.

The partners do the form in the opposite direction with roles reversed.

Do the form on both sides.

The form can be done with focus, with slight impact, as a 'plant and push' drill, and so on.

When the partners have the form down they can add a second punch in each position and utilize the buddha palm block (guard the face) prior to each regular strike.

Having students drill this form endlessly will replace the basic forms, such as kebons or taikyoku, and result in much more certainty and effectiveness with the basic blocks.

Drilling this form will prepare the students for freestyle quite rapidly.

Drilling the two man form with a partner obviates the need for doing individual applications form the form.

Chapter Four
Matrixing

Matrixing is the science of the martial arts. It is logical, it makes sense, and it makes everything easier, and therefore faster, to learn.

I used make long lists of techniques, trying to put them together in one list so that I could have all my arts in order. Except that things got too big, too complex, so I was forced to figure out a different way of listing techniques. Matrixing became the logical method because it allowed me to see all the techniques in one simple graph. Except the graphs got too big, and I started focusing on the concepts. When I started focusing on concepts it was like the key to the door had been turned, the door was opened, and everything became simple dimple and easy to figure out. On the following page is an example of one of my first matrixes.

	low	high	outward	inward
low	low/low	low/high	low/out	low/in
high	high/low	high/high	high/out	high/in
outward	out/low	out/high	out/out	out/in
inward	in/low	in/high	in/out	in/in

This would be a blocking matrix from Karate. The good news is that every technique, based on the four basic blocks, is included. It is very easy to go through them and make a list of them in the right order, simple to difficult. The more good news is that this matrix enabled me to see how many blocks were not included in the classical line up, therefore revealing why the classical had become inadequate as a teaching method. Which enabled me to better teach my own arts, and better able to create better arts.

I began writing matrixes for different sets of blocks, for different types of blocks, and even was able to easily create matrixes for blocks from different arts. This last showed how arts were not able to be combined easily as the concepts become opposing.

I matrixed such concepts as time in the martial arts, space in the martial arts, the architecture (geometry) of systems, and so on.

Eventually the matrixes gave way to a new study: Neutronics, which is the philosophy, or the science behind the science of the martial arts.

At this point I had successfully solved the 'puzzle' of the martial arts. I began to create new arts, trying to make an art that would include all the concepts and techniques I had learned, and in a simple to learn and logical format. And this led to the art you hold in your hand, 'Nine Square Diagram Boxing.'

Nine Square Diagram Boxing had to meet several conditions to be considered good and viable.

> It had to be founded on Basic-Basics.
> It had to be structured on basics.
> It had to be logical and scientific.
> It had to be simple.
> It had to include a progression from strikes to take downs.
> It had to include every range of the body.
> It had to be in simple modules (forms), as in Pa Kua Chang.
> The modules (forms) had to be interchangeable.
> The modules (forms) had to be matrixable.
> It had to have a small number of techniques.
> The techniques had to progress from soft to hard.
> It had to be teachable as Tai Chi, but easily adapted to Karate.
> The techniques had to be matrixable.
> It had to be adaptable to weapons training.
> There could be no missing pieces.
> Everything had to adhere to the logic of matrixing.
> Everything had to manifest the philosophy of Neutronics.

There were more conditions, but these were the most important.

And, I have to say, the art you hold in your hands succeeded on all these counts.

36

Chapter Five
Second Basic Form

Below are the videos for the nine square basic forms.

9 square double out
https://youtu.be/HLBV23HTGb0

9 square X low
https://youtu.be/brbZJyvq_Uw

9 9 square X hi wrist
https://youtu.be/2xhVUP_A8sM

HOUSE TWO

1   Attacker steps forward with the left foot and punches with the right hand.

Defender steps back with the right foot into a front stance and executes a low crossed wrist block.

2   Attacker punches with the left hand.

Defender shifts/steps back with the left foot into a back stance as he executes a left inward middle block.

3   Defender shifts/steps forward with the left foot into a front stance as he executes a right punch.

4	Attacker steps forward with the right foot into a front stance and swings the right sword hand downward like a sword.

Defender steps back with the left foot into a back stance as he executes a high crossed wrist block.

5	Attacker punches with the left hand.

Defender executes a right outward middle block.

6	Defender shifts/steps forward with the right foot into a front stance as he executes a left punch.

7   The attacker steps forward with the left foot and pushes to the chest with two hands.

The defender steps back with the right foot into a back stance and executes double outward middle grabs.

8   Attacker punches with the right hand.

Defender executes a left cross palm block and a left front kick to the high inside thigh of the attacker's rear leg.

9   Defender sets the left foot down gently in a back stance as he executes a right punch.

10   Defender shifts/pivots/ steps into horse stance as he executes a left horizontal elbow strike.

11   The defender becomes the attacker and pivots into a front stance and punches to the groin with the right hand.

The attacker becomes the defender as he executes a low crossed wrist block.

The form is then done in the opposite direction with the attacker as defender and defender as attacker.

Drilling the two man form with a partner obviates the need for doing individual applications form the form.

Past the Two Man House form we will be going into three and four strike applications.

Chapter Six
The Full Matrix

On the following page is the full matrix of eight basic blocks. I usually have a person work with the previous matrix, the four basic blocks shown in the previous graph, until they have done the two House forms. Then I have them work on the full matrix.

The way to do this techniques is to have one person step forward and punch twice. For instance, lo/lo, or lo hi, or low out, and so on through the matrix.

The defender steps back so that the body is aligned for the first block, then does a simple triangle step to the side to do the second block.

	lo	hi	out	in	x-low	x-hi	palm	inv lo
lo	lo lo	lo hi	lo out	lo in	lo x-lo	lo x-hi	lo palm	lo inv lo
hi	hi lo	hi hi	hi out	hi in	hi x-lo	hi x-hi	hi palm	hi inv lo
out	out lo	out hi	out out	out in	out x-lo	out x-hi	out palm	out inv lo
in	in lo	in hi	in out	in in	in x-lo	in x-hi	in palm	in inv lo
x-lo	x-lo lo	x-lo hi	x-lo out	x-lo in	x-lo x-lo	x-lo x-hi	x-lo palm	x-lo inv lo
x-hi	x-hi lo	x-hi hi	x-hi out	x-hi in	x-hi x-lo	x-hi x-hi	x-hi palm	x-hi inv lo
palm	palm lo	palm hi	palm out	palm in	palm x-lo	palm x-hi	palm palm	palm inv lo
inv lo	inv lo lo	inv lo hi	inv lo out	inv lo in	inv lo x-lo	inv lo x-hi	inv lo palm	inv lo inv lo

THE TRIANGLE STEP

Begin in a back stance with
 with the right foot forward.

Step back and to the right
with the right foot.

Bring the left foot in and
forward so that you are in
a back stance on the other
side.

You will find that
students tend to shuffle their
feet forward and back.

You must make them
move sideways, so they are
moving off the line of
attack.

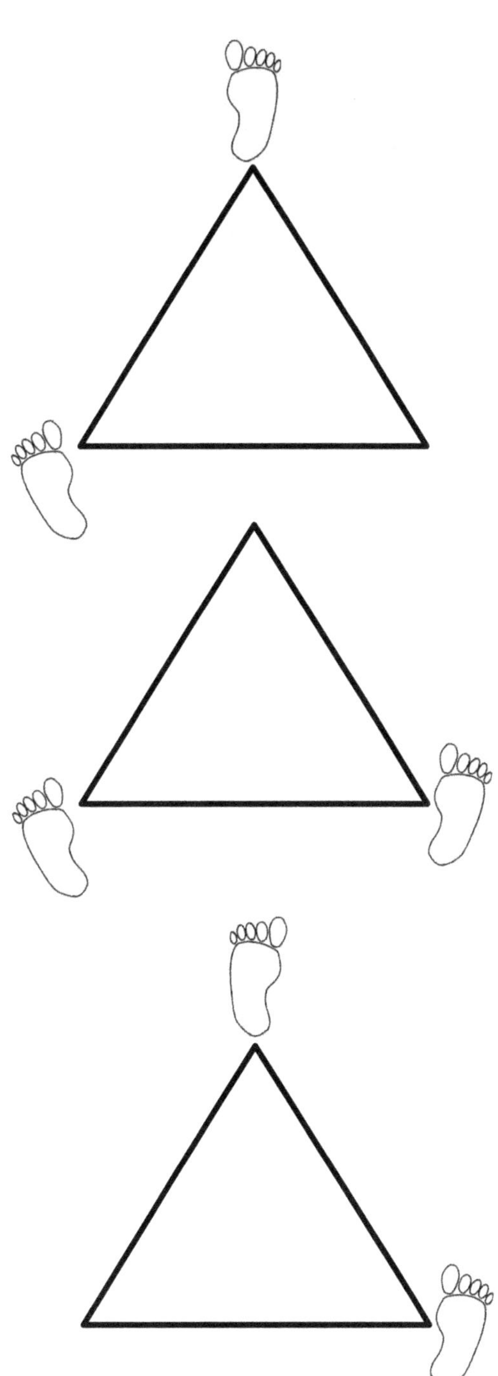

Chapter Seven
Footwork Diagram,
Intermediate Forms and Lop Sau

Below is the videos for this section.

9 sq footwork.mp4
https://youtu.be/TnYfcprlnks

9 square low high.mp4
https://youtu.be/0SQvMDQSyV4

9 square mid high
https://youtu.be/LM9eTxmvMtY

9 square combining form
https://youtu.be/2XZNBeHOvfE

14 9 square lop sau
https://youtu.be/-3SfVd8JMys

THE DIAGRAM

I use the House forms for teaching basics that actually work. This totally replaces early basic block forms taught in most arts.

One should be able to do a solo form when one doesn't have a partner. But punching the air is no substitute for punching a real, live body. One must learn what it feels like, what one has to do to make the art work, and dozens of other things.

I usually teach House One and Two as quickly as the student can absorb them. Which means as soon as the student can go through the first form, I start teaching him the second form.

After the student has both the house forms down to an intuitive level, and this happens fast if you push the Basic-Basics, I put them on the Diagram.

There are 9 techniques, which mean 9 forms. Though, to be honest, the number of potential forms is limited only by the imagination.

Sometimes students will find the forms boring…until the student has reached a certain degree of understanding. Once the student has broken through the plateau of boredom he/she will find a depth of understanding and spirit they didn't know existed.

I usually show the forms slow style, as if doing Tai Chi Chuan. After the student shows a degree of understanding I show him other ways of doing the forms, and this includes a slow circle and pulse to a snap, hard karate style, kung fu concepts, and so on.

To expect a form to be done only one way is silly. A form should be explored not just for a plethora of applications, but for a wide variety of timing and flow. It should also be done on both sides, backwards, with weapons in the hands, and so on.

I don't go into footworks such as Foursquare, or triangular (except in technical applications). I do play with circle walking, especially in two man drills.

Here is the Nine Square Diagram.

There are 9 squares. There are 20 counts. One steps through 13 squares on a figure eight pattern.

One can obviously find and use different geometries on the Nine Square Diagram, but it is recommended that you master the basics moves described on the pages of this book before doing so.

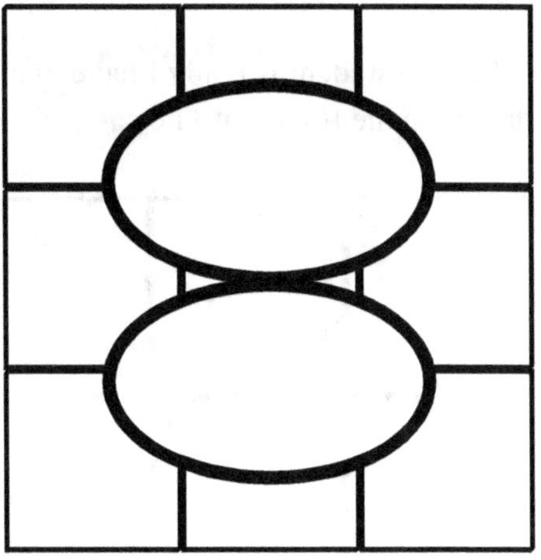

THE NINE SQUARE DIAGRAM

Here is the Nine Square Diagram Form done for the technique called 'Roll Back.'

When the student is ready I have him walk on a numbered diagram, drawn on the floor, until he can walk on a diagram without numbers.

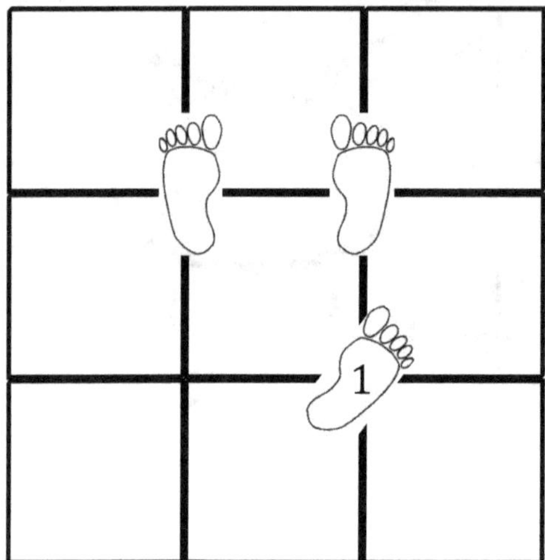

1 Step back with the right foot into a right back stance.

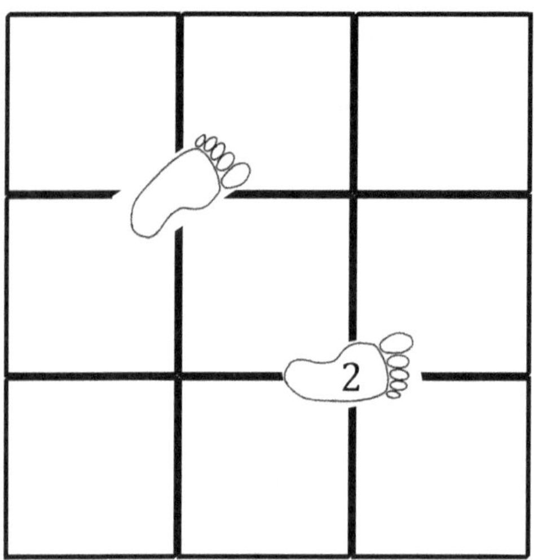

2 Pivot to the right into a left back stance.

3 Step back with the right foot to a right back stance.

4 Pivot to the right into a left back stance.

5 Step back with the right foot into a right back stance.

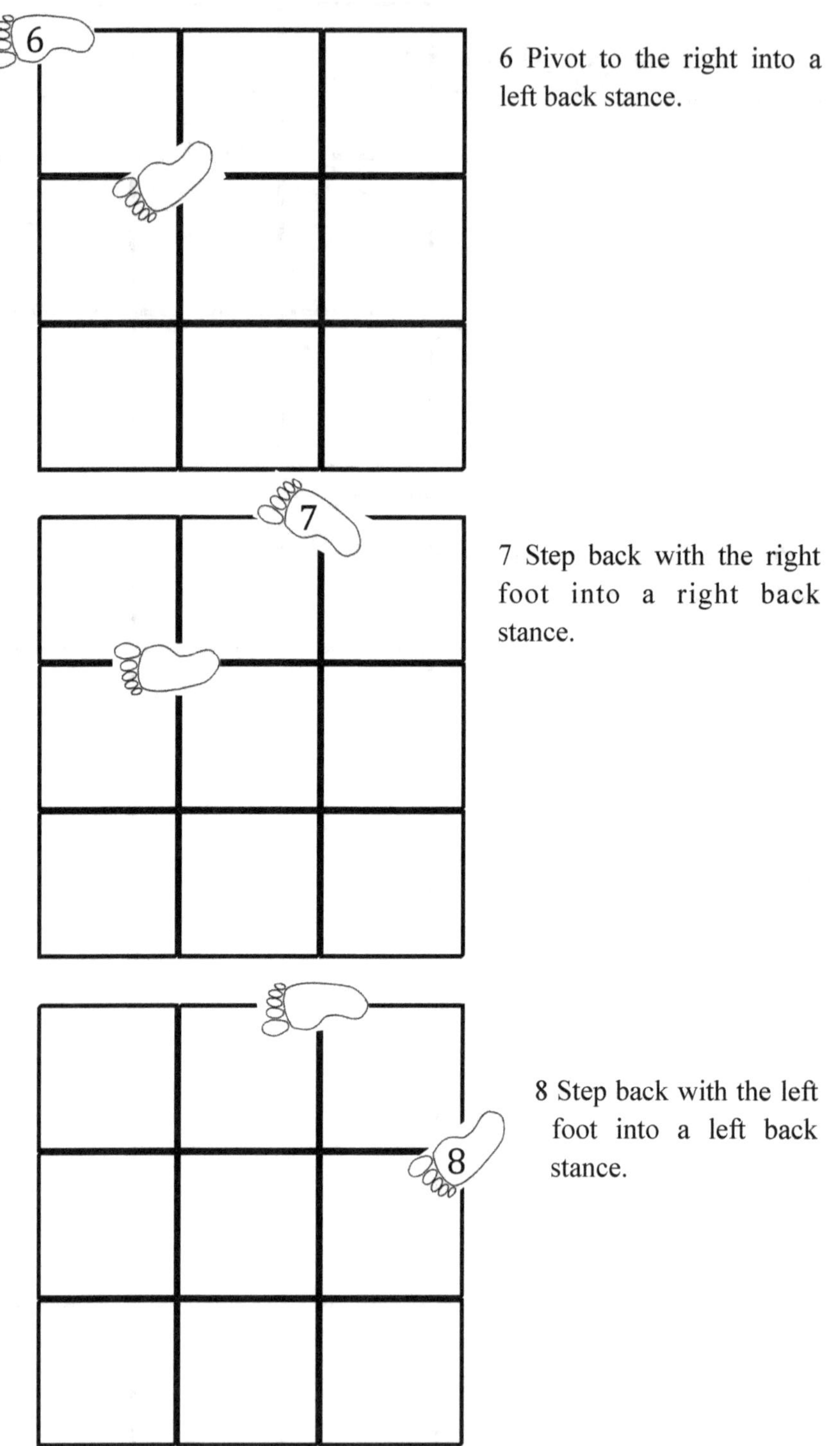

6 Pivot to the right into a left back stance.

7 Step back with the right foot into a right back stance.

8 Step back with the left foot into a left back stance.

9 Step to the left, in front of the right foot, and pivot to the left into a right back stance.

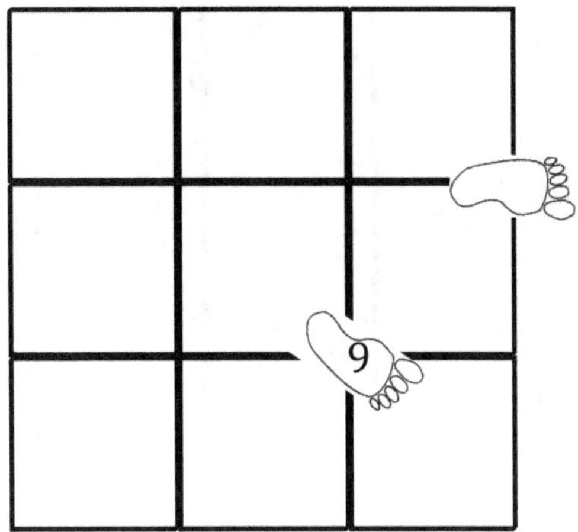

10 Step back with the left foot into a left back stance.

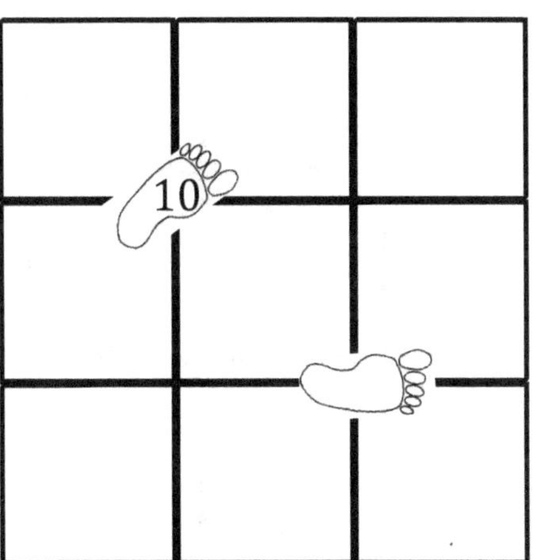

11 Step back with the right foot into a right back stance.

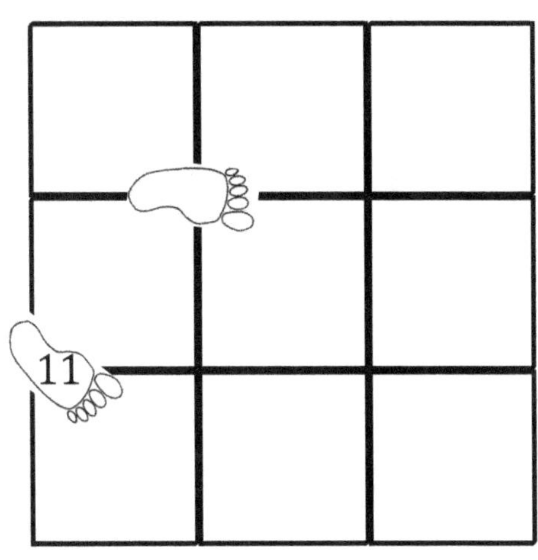

12 Step to the right in front of the right foot with the left foot into a right back stance.

13 Step back with the right foot into a right back stance.

14 Step back with the left foot into a left back stance.

15 Pivot to the left into a right back stance.

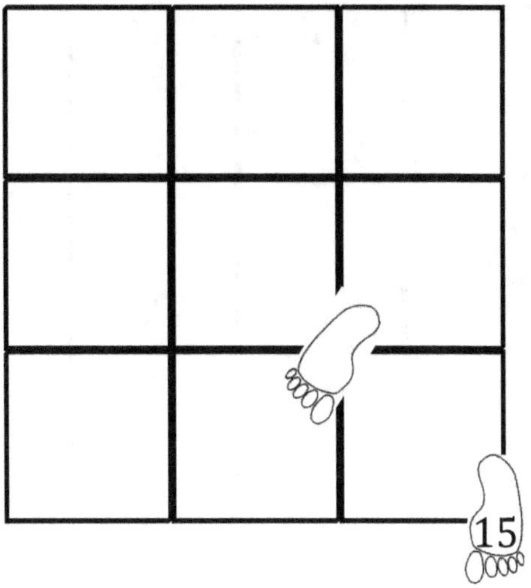

16 Step back with the left foot into a left back stance.

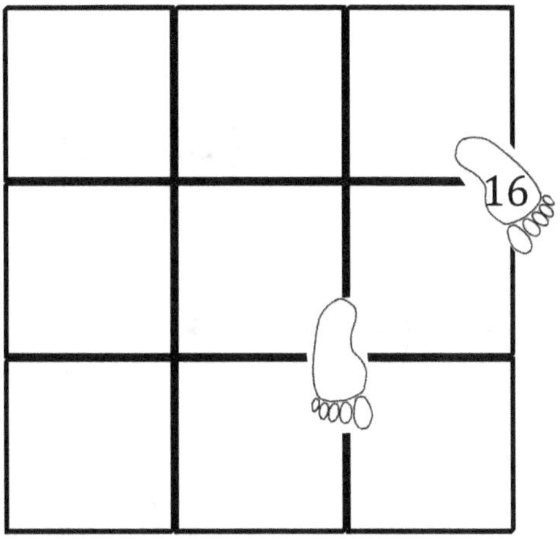

17 Pivot to the left into a right back stance.

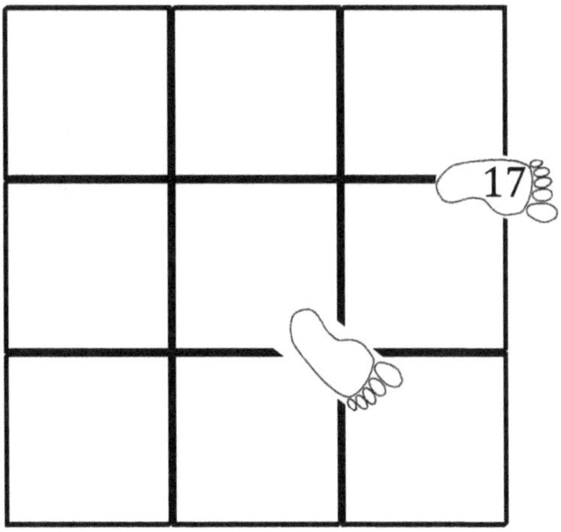

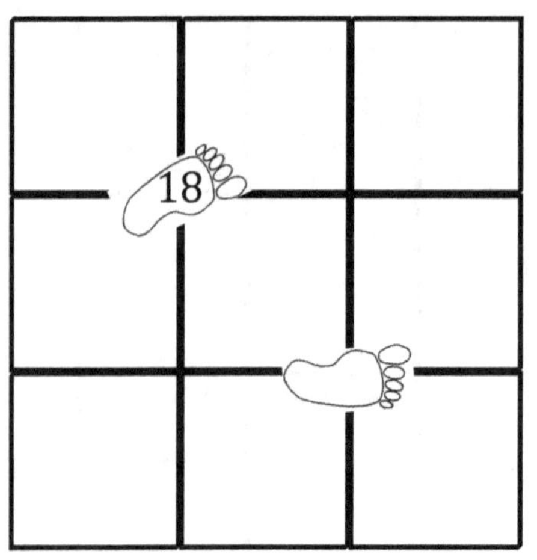

18 Step back with the left foot into a left back stance.

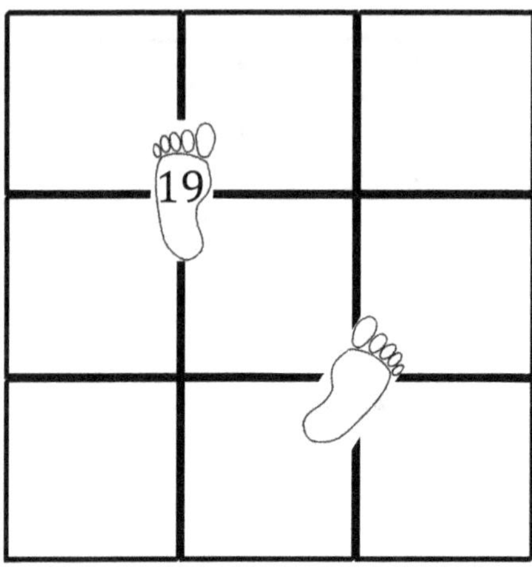

19 Pivot to the left into right back stance.

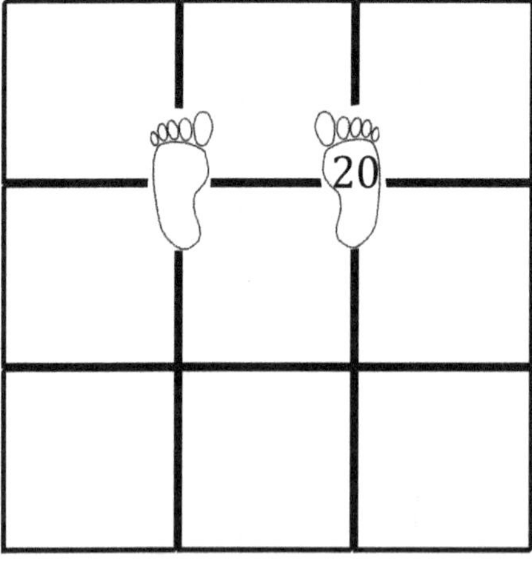

20 Bring the right foot forward to a natural stance at the starting position.

The Nine Square Diagram is a simple means of learning the basic footwork. One can always create other patterns if they wish to explore other footworks, adapt techniques to different directions, and so on.

Most forms with have a basic technique which is repeated through all the steps. This usually includes shifting into a front stance right after assuming the back stance.

One must pay close attention to the turn of feet and hips so that the body is always properly aligned.

Do not not pivot on a weight leg as that can, eventually, damage the knee. Take the weight off, then pivot.

58

Chapter Eight
Roll Back/Brush Knee

Below are the videos for this section.

Roll Back/Brush Knee
https://youtu.be/fyO8yncBhVw

ROLL BACK

The first form, or module, or diagram is based on 'Roll Back/Brush Knee,' as described in Tai Chi Chuan. You will find a certain progression of art in this form that expands it far beyond just Tai Chi, and a full range of applicable techniques.

The best way to teach this form is to have the student walk the numbered squares, as previously described. When he has the footwork down simply show him the technique of roll back, walk him through a couple of squares, then tell him to just plug the handwork into the footwork. People become extremely proficient very quickly using this method.

On the following page is the basic move.

0 Assume a standing position.

1 Step back with the right foot as you move the right hand inward as a slap.

2 Turn the hips to the right and you sink back on the right foot in a back stance. The right arm pulls back and the left arm circles to the front. It should feel like pulling a rope.

3 Move the right hand in as you turn the hips to the left (squaring them) and shift forward into a front stance. The right arm executes a palm strike to the front.

Now do the Roll Back move on the nine square. Just follow the footwork and plug in the Roll Back move. On the next page I will detail the form step by step. We won't do this for the other forms, as everything should be self explanatory once you've gone through this form.

For later practice, once you have the form down (or once your student has the form down), you can show the student other ways to do the form. For instance, one can slow the movements and pulse them to finally explode with a fist. This involves isolating each body part, pushing with the leg, turning the hip, rotating the shoulder, and finally pumping the punch. See the image below.

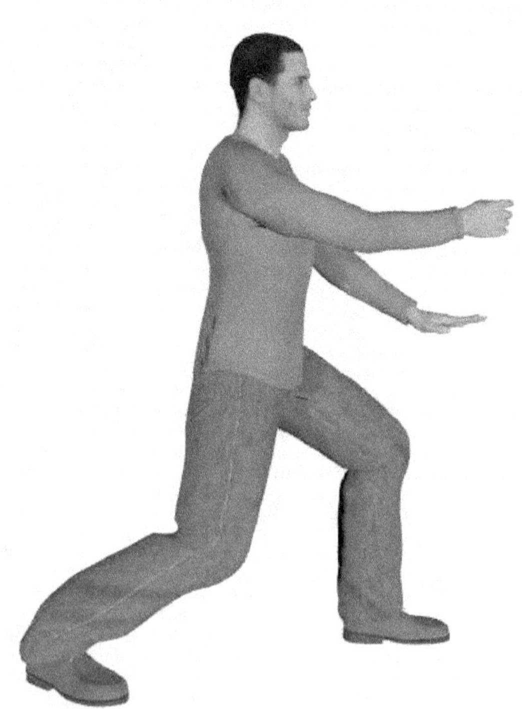

NINE SQUARE DIAGRAM
ROLL BACK FORM

Stand on the front of the middle square in a natural stance.

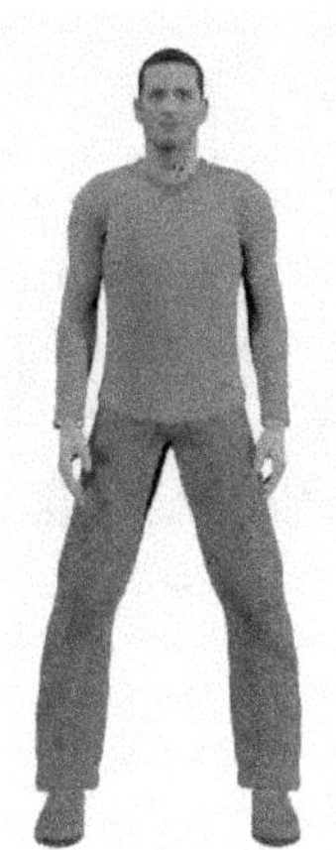

Step back with the right foot as you execute a right slap.

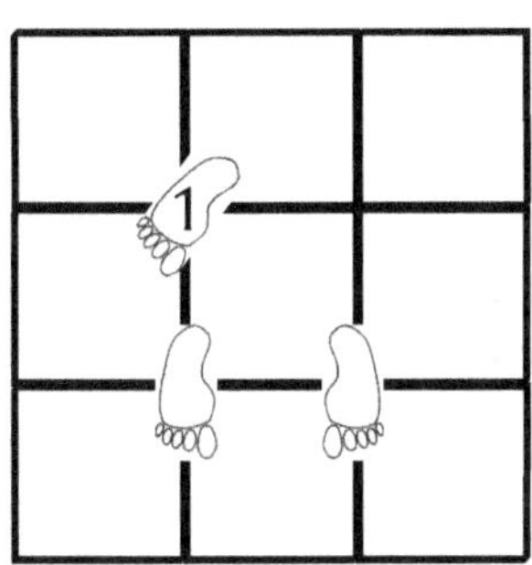

Pivot to the right into a back stance as you execute 'Roll Back.'

The back stance may seem a bit wide. You can always tighten it up if you wish.

Circle the left arm down and pulse the right palm into a front stance 'Brush Knee.'

Pivot to the right as you execute a right low block and a left palm block.

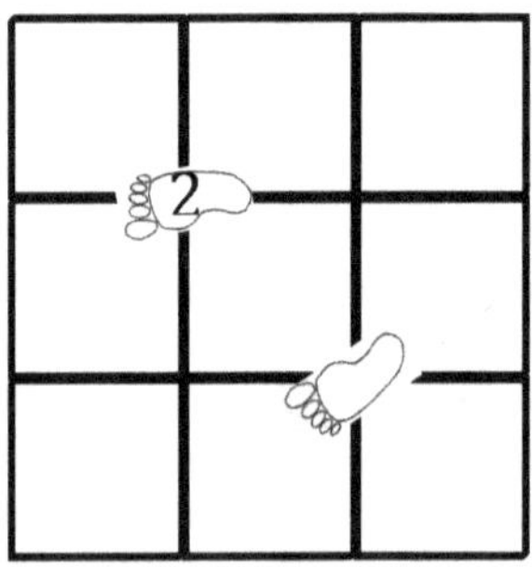
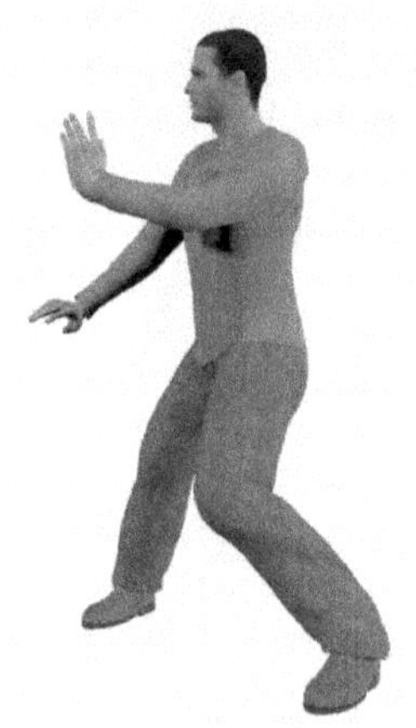

Assume a back stance as you make the palm block into a left slap.

Pivot to the left as you execute a 'Roll Back.'

Pay close attention to the hip changes. The hips create a line between the feet and the hand.

Shift into a front stance as you execute a 'Brush Knee.'

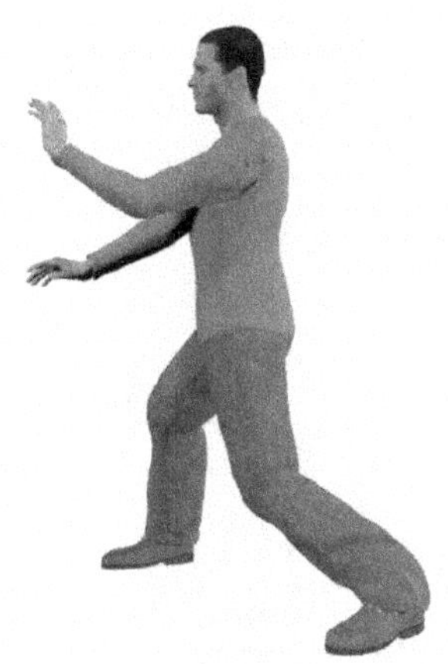

Step back with the right foot as you execute a right slap.

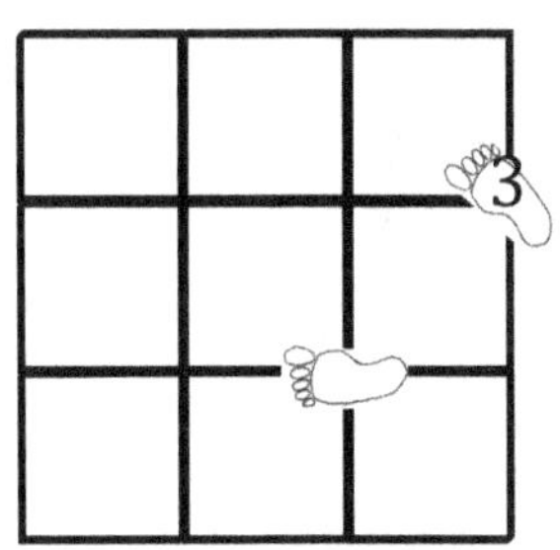

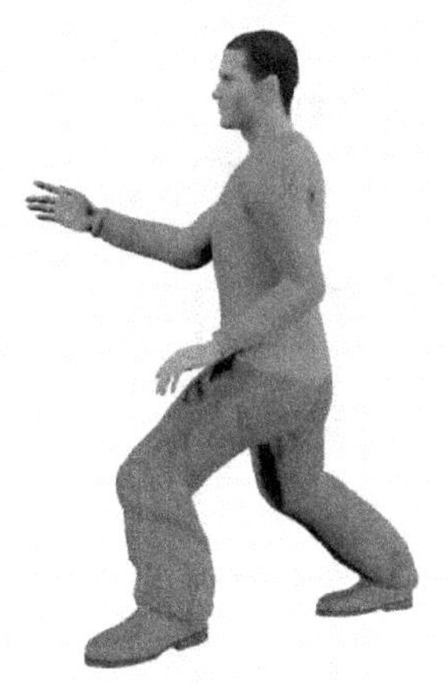

Pivot to the right as you execute 'Roll Back.'

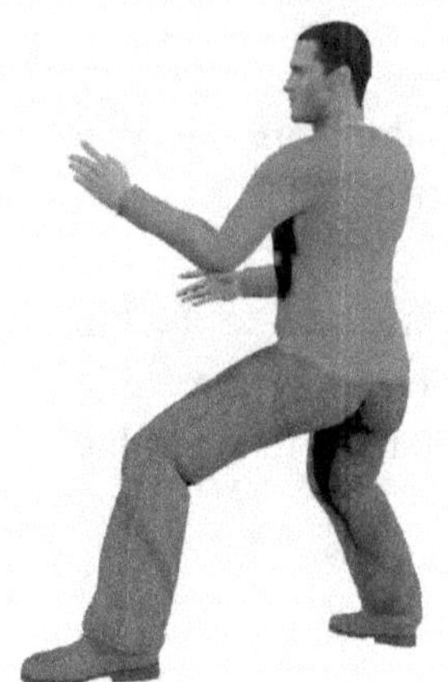

Shift forward into a front stance as you execute 'Brush Knee.'

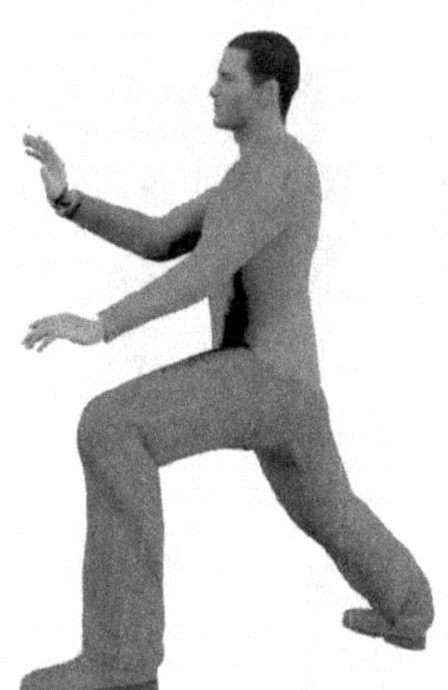

Pivot to the right with a right low block and a left palm block (that becomes a slap).

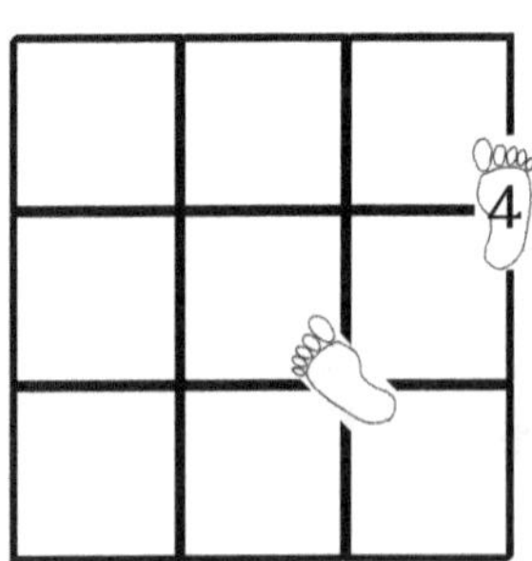

Pivot to the right as you execute 'Roll Back.'

Shift into a front stance as you execute 'Brush Knee.'

Step back with the right foot as you execute a right slap.

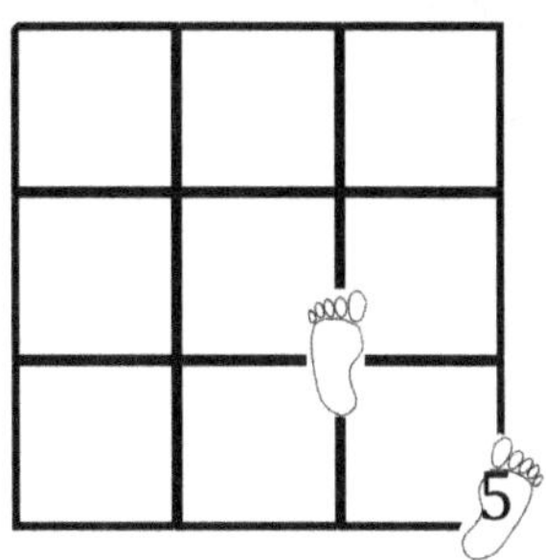

Pivot to the right into a back stance as you execute 'Roll Back.'

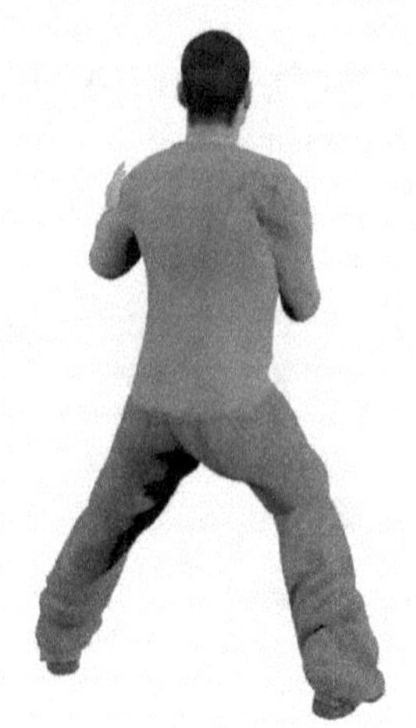

Shift into a front stance as you execute 'Brush Knee.'

Pivot to the right with a right low block and a left palm block (which becomes a slap).

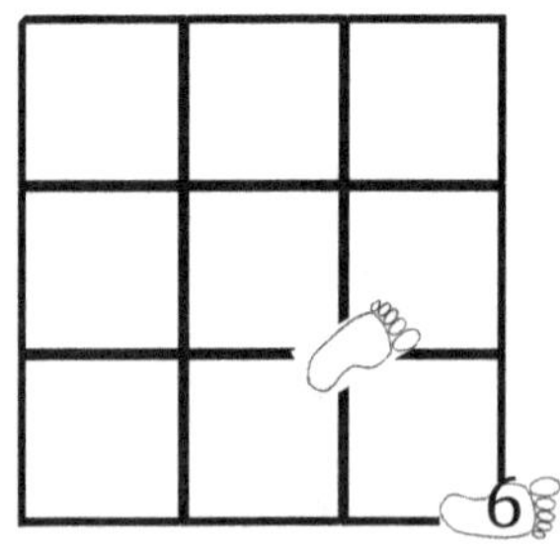

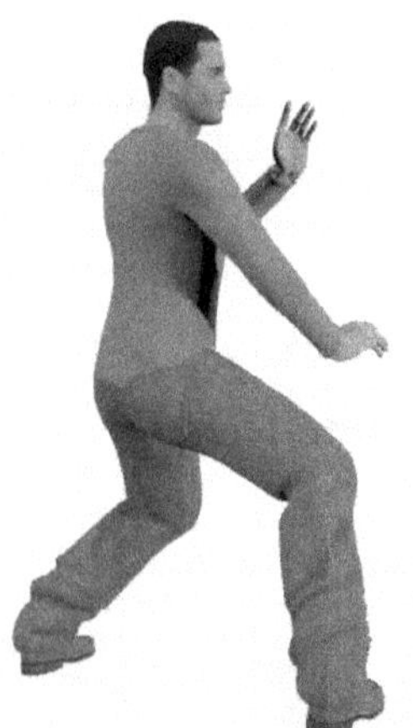

Pivot to the left into a back stance as you execute 'Roll Back.'

Shift into a front stance as you execute 'Brush Knee.'

Step back with the right foot as you execute a right slap.

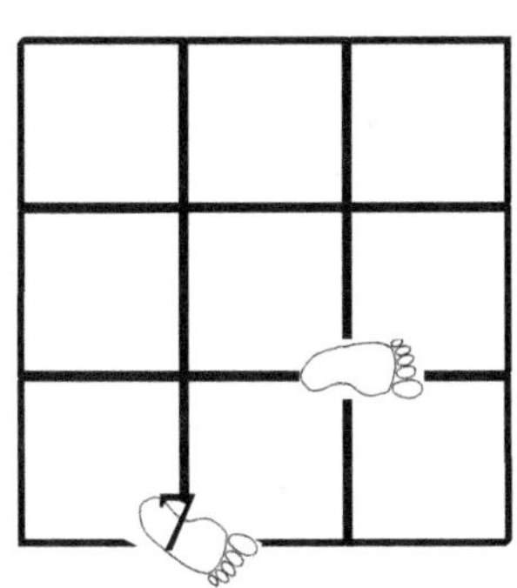

Pivot to the right into a back stance as you execute 'Roll Back.'

Shift into a front stance as you execute 'Brush Knee.'

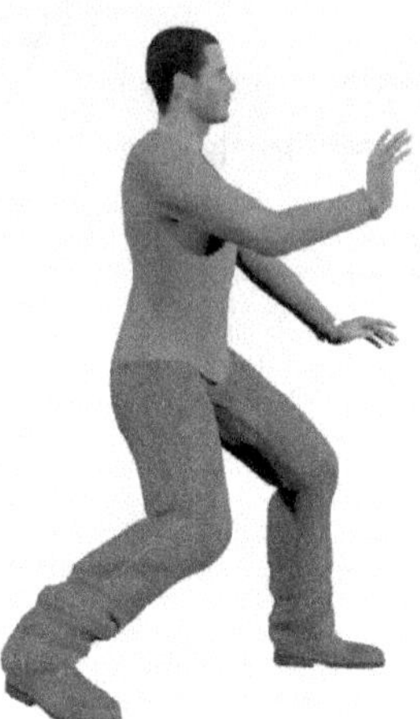

Step back with the left foot as you execute a left slap.

Pivot to the left into a back stance as you execute 'Roll Back.'

Shift into a front stance as you execute 'Brush Knee.'

Step to the left with your right foot and turn 180 degrees with a left low block and a right palm block (which turns into a slap).

Pivot to the right into a back stance as you execute 'Roll Back.'

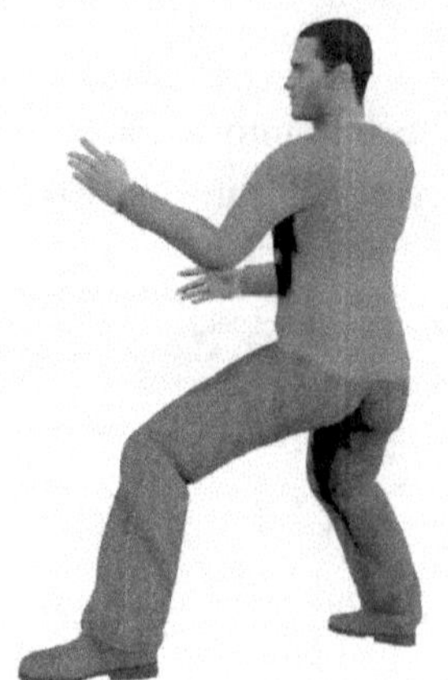

Shift into a front stance as you execute 'Brush Knee.'

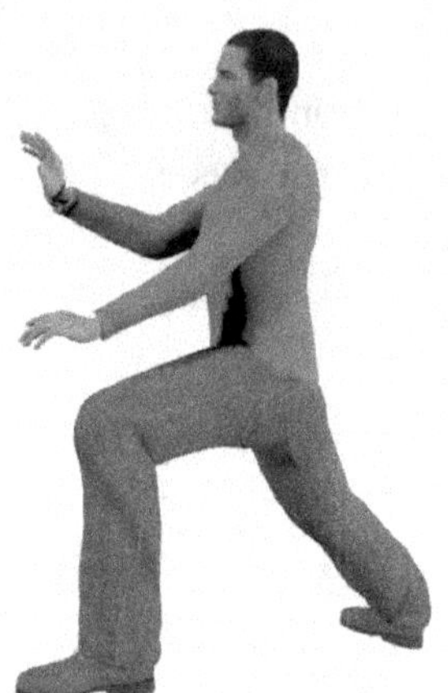

Step back with the left foot as you execute a left slap.

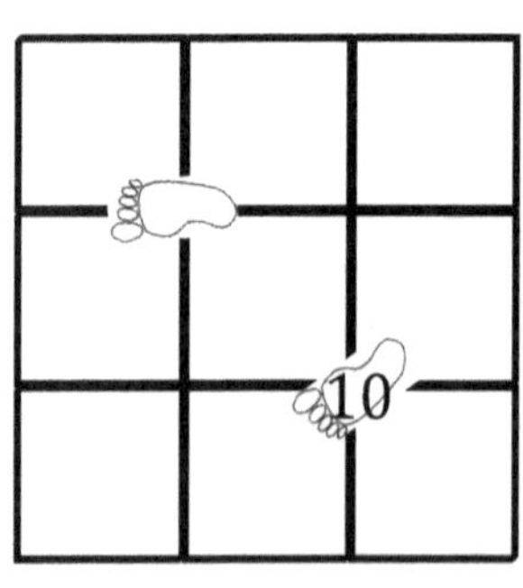

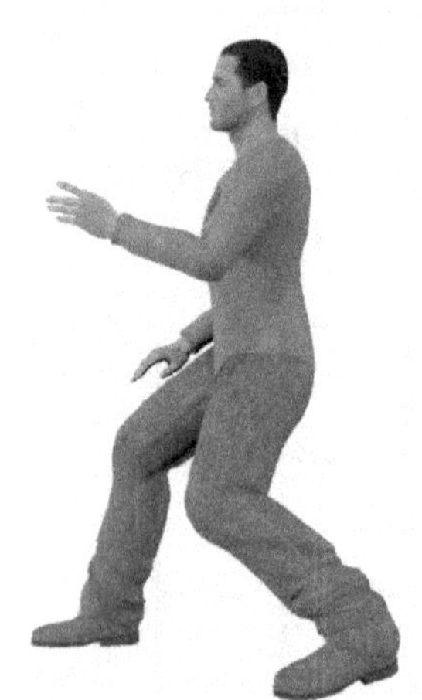

Pivot to the left into a back stance as you execute 'Roll Back.'

Shift into a front stance as you execute 'Brush Knee.'

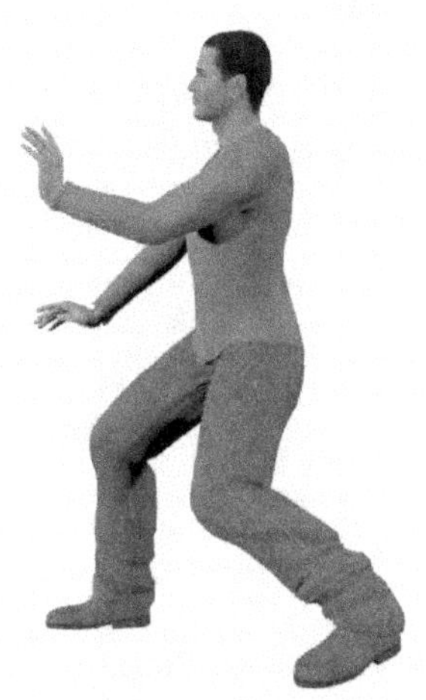

Step back with the right foot as you execute a right slap.

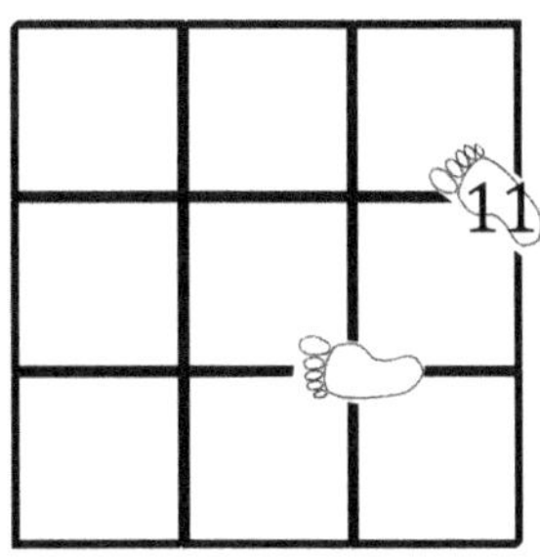

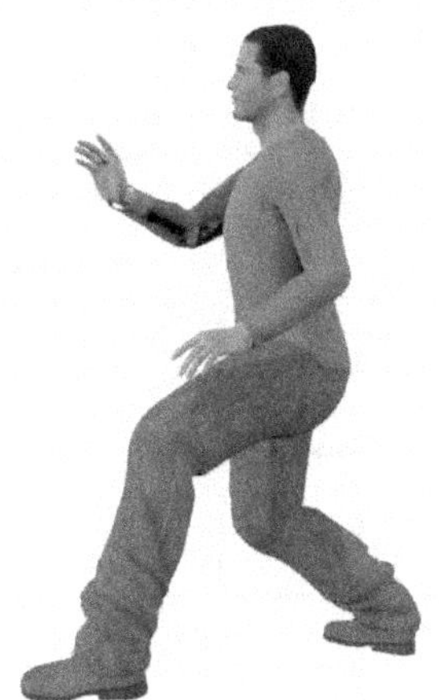

Pivot to the right into a back stance as you execute 'Roll Back.'

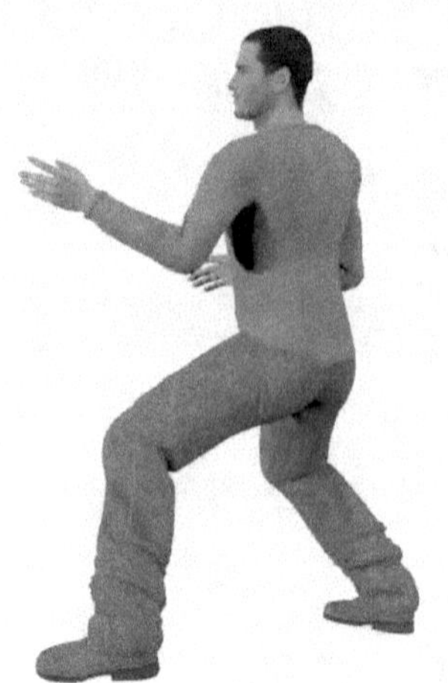

Shift into a front stance as you execute 'Brush Knee.'

Step to the right with the left foot and turn 180 degrees with a right low block and a left palm block (which becomes a slap).

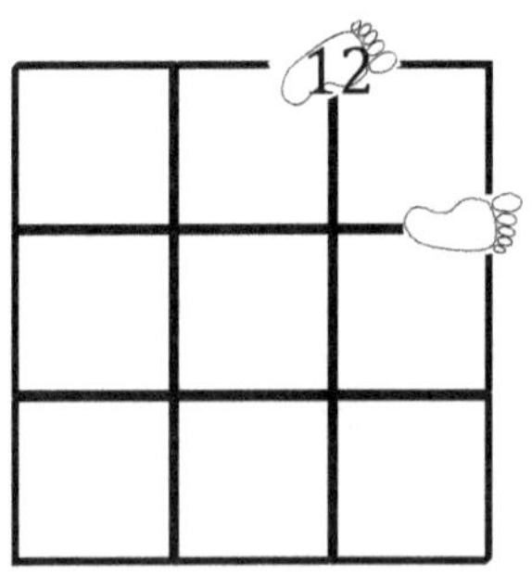

Pivot to the left into a back stance as you execute Roll Back.

Shift into a front stance as you execute 'Brush Knee.'

Step back with the right foot as you execute a right slap.

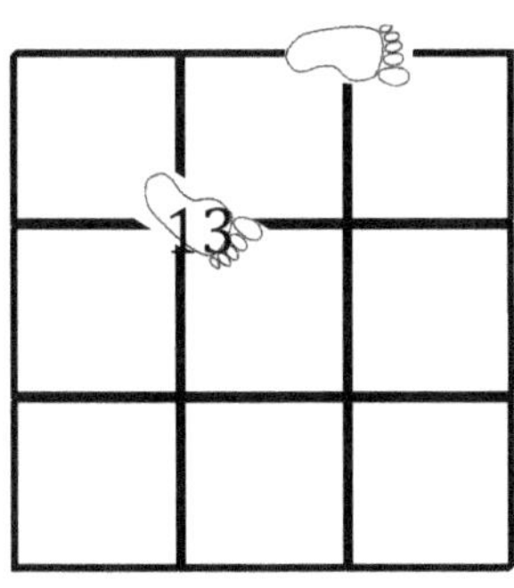

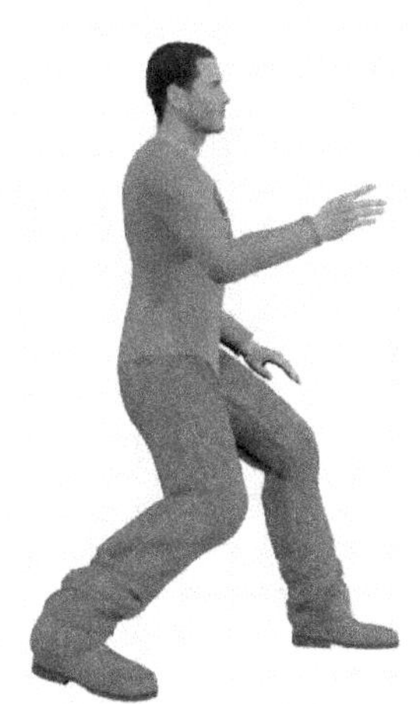

Pivot to the right into a back stance as you execute 'Roll Back.'

Shift into a front stance as you execute 'Brush Knee.'

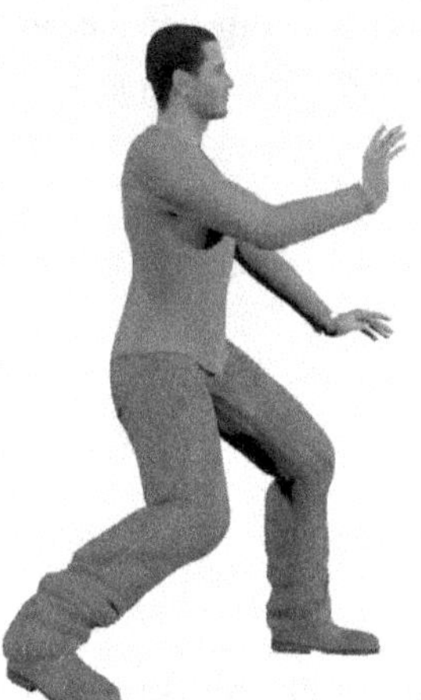

Step back with the left foot as you execute a left slap.

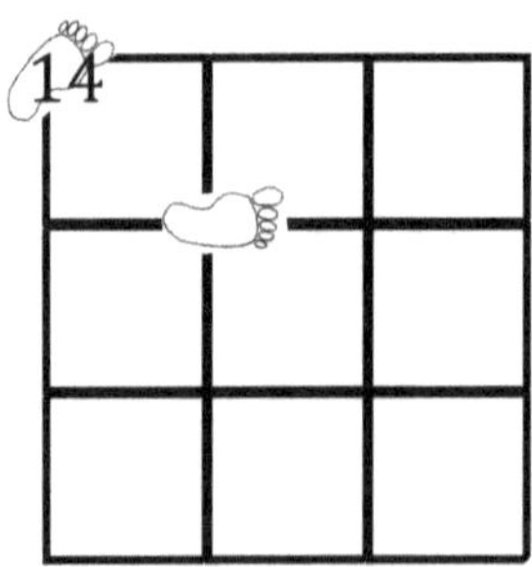

Pivot to the left into a back stance as you execute 'Roll Back.'

Shift into a front stance as you execute 'Brush Knee.'

Pivot to the left as you execute a left low block and a right palm block (which becomes a slap).

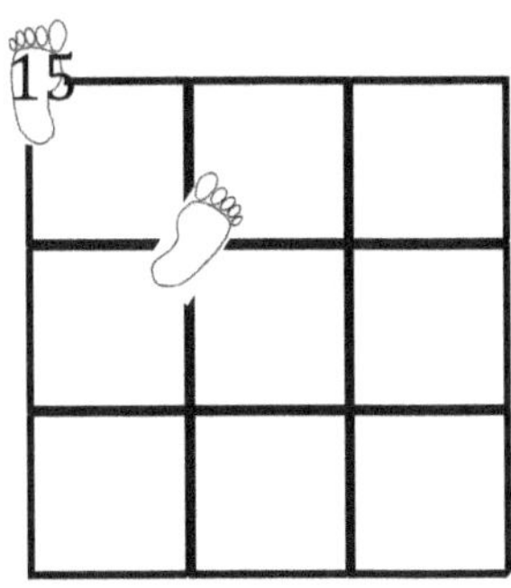

Pivot to the right into a back stance as you execute 'Roll Back.'

Shift into a front stance as you execute 'Brush Knee.'

Step back with the left foot as you execute a left slap.

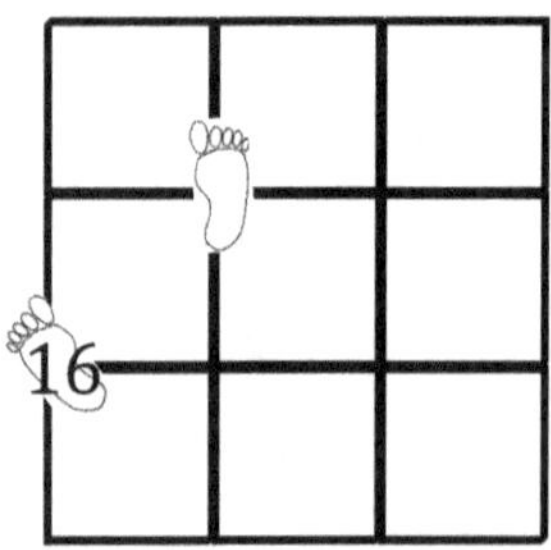

Pivot to the left into a back stance as you execute 'Roll Back.'

Shift into a front stance as you execute 'Brush Knee.'

Pivot to the left with a left low block and a right palm block (which turns into a slap).

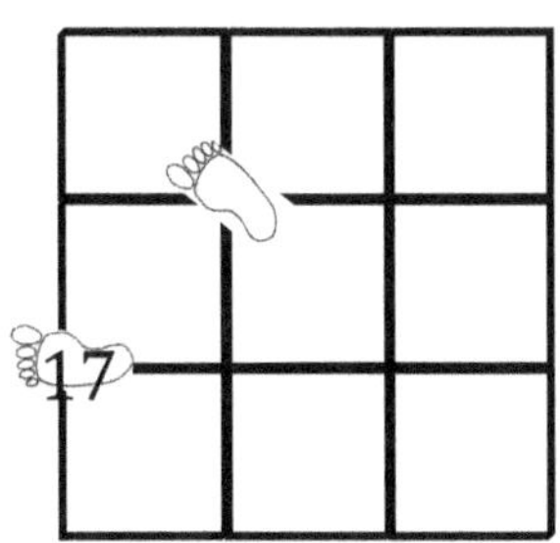

Pivot to the right into a back stance as you execute 'Roll Back.'

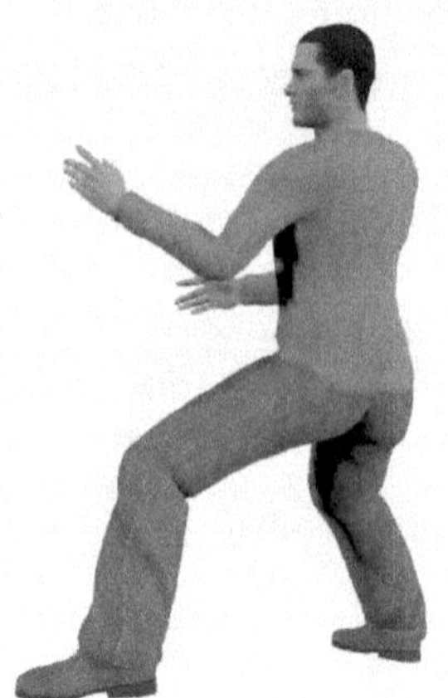

Shift into a front stance as you execute 'Brush Knee.'

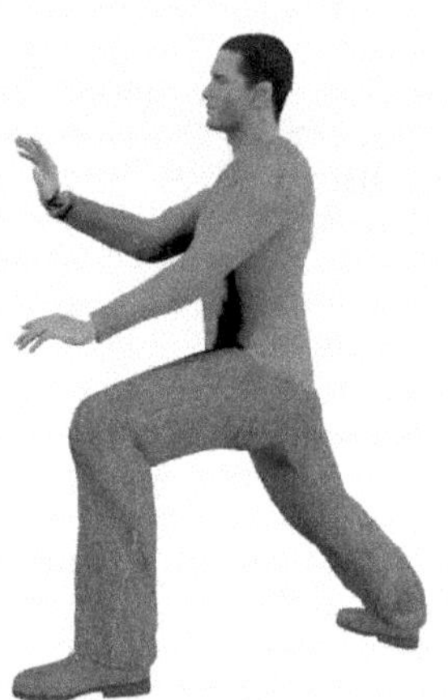

Step back with the left foot as you execute a left slap.

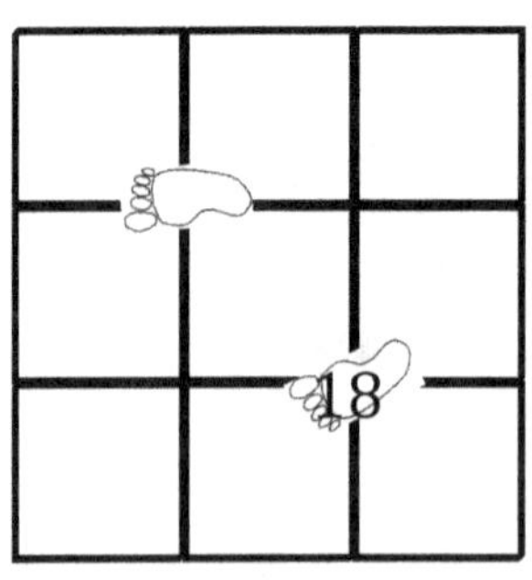

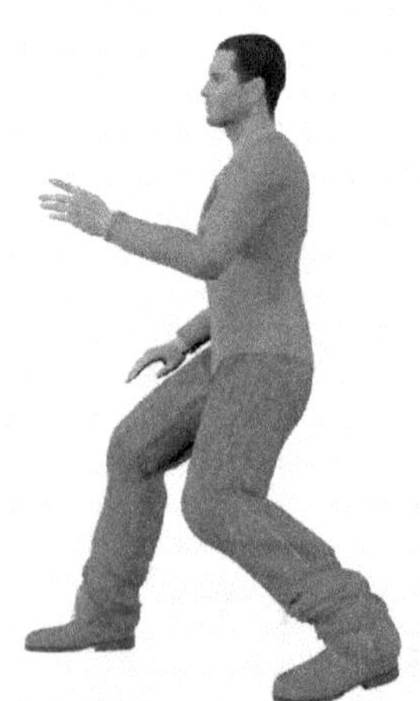

Pivot to the left as you execute a left low block and a right palm block (which becomes a slap).

Pivot to the right into a back stance as you execute 'Roll Back.'

Shift into a front stance as you execute 'Brush Knee.'

Step forward with the right foot to a natural stance in the starting position.

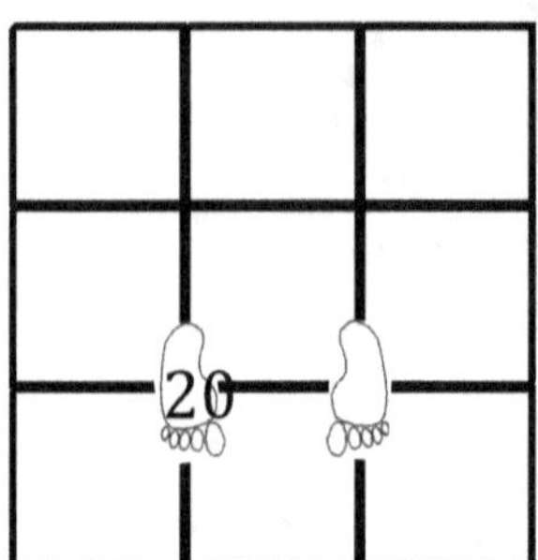

Remember, this is usually taught tai chi style. When a person has the footwork done, introduce the handwork. When the handwork is adequate introduce concepts from other arts. show the student how to block and strike, as in karate. Show him how to pulse the body and snap the fist, as in forms of Kung Fu.

I particularly like doing this form with my eyes closed. If you end up in the beginning position, even though your eyes are closed, you will have a better ability to understand your position in space.

I will not walk you through the whole forms from this point on. I will just show you the basic technique and you are expected to plug the technique into the Nine Square just as you did this last form.

Incidentally, in the next section we will be doing 'Promise Fights.' These are form applications, but I prefer the term 'Promise Fight' because it means you must understand the promise of a fight, you must understand the idea behind the form or the application.

ROLL BACK
PROMISE FIGHTS

There are many Promise Fights, or form applications, for each of the Nine Square techniques.

In the first technique the attacker and defender face each other at 'handshake' distance apart.

The attacker steps back with the right foot into a front stance with the right hand ready to strike and the left hand in the downward position. This is the starting position for all Promised fights. This position allows the defender to see the attack coming, and to start the analysis process.

The attacker steps forward with the right foot and strikes to the chest. The defender steps back with the left foot and slaps the punch inward (closing) with his left hand.

The attacker punches with the left hand. The defender assumes the Roll Back position and slaps the punch inward (closing) with his right hand.

The defender brushes the attacker's left fist downward and to the side with his right low block as he shuffles forward and places a palm on the attacker's chest.

Doing the technique this way accomplishes two things.

First, one learns how to block single punches by doing the House forms. This technique begins the matrixing of blocking two (or more) strikes. This is very important if the student ever expects to develop true intuition and be able to 'think' (know what is happening as it happens) in the middle of a technique.

Second, one can develop 'plant and push' with the palm on the chest. If you can gently push a person's whole weight, you can snap a fist and punch with your whole weight.

And, one can obviously do this with a snap of the left hand into a fist, more karate style, and creating impact. The impact should be like knocking on a door, you want to hear the vibration go through the whole house, or body.

The matrix for 'two strikes' is not a graph, but a simple list. I call it the Matrix for Two Strikes.

close the right punch	close the left punch
close the right punch	open the left punch
open the right punch	close the left punch
open the right punch	open the left punch

The promise fights for the Nine Square techniques explore this matrix thoroughly.

This is a roll back application from Tai Chi. Catch the arm by the wrist and the elbow. Make sure the wrist, the elbow and the shoulders are in a straight line. Lower the wrist so that the shoulder raises, then move forward and push.

Starting with distance, and moving the bodies in the same direction in the beginning of the technique trains the defender on how to analyze distance, and therefore to control distance.

When one does things Tai Chi style, or wants to learn 'pulsing,' they should push first with the leg, turn (or straighten) the hips, push with the arms.

In this promise fight Roll back is done on the opposite side, opening the opponent. This should be done with snap as it is a karate style inward block. Then simply punch with the left hand. Or jab with the front fingers, or kick with the front leg.

Which brings us to the point of it all.

The three promise fights I have shown you have demonstrated three items.

First, to block two strikes inward (closing).

Second, to do the move Tai Chi style by absorbing and repelling.

Third, to do the technique Karate style by blocking and punching.

And, you can doubtless see how these three simple techniques can be mixed and matched. Do the double slap inward and then punch. Slap one block and catch the next one to turn the fellow, break his elbow, thrust him backward, and so on.

This is all the tip of the iceberg. Consider the next section.

Chapter Nine
Matrixing Six Directions

There are six directions. Seven if you consider holding your position as a direction. Holding your position in a fight is incredibly important, and could even be considered the hallmark of the true art. Holding one's position gives one power; to the degree that one does not hold his position one does not have power.

The essence of a study of true karate results in somebody being able to hold a specific position in space, to have the power when not to hold a position, and to direct an attack (control it) in any of the six directions.

The six directions are: up, down, left, right, back, forward. Thus, simply speaking, you can force or flow an attack upwards. You can block or guide an attack downwards. You can push an attacker's arm across his body (closing him), or push it out from his body (opening him. You can step backwards, creating space for the opponent to 'fall' into, or move forward, jamming the technique.

Obviously, force or flow will be possible to varying degree for each direction, and one must practice a range of blocking to giving way.

One can utilize the six directions in one's body motion, in conjunction with one's arms, the direction you 'launch' the attacker in, and so on.

You have done three techniques. These techniques push backward with force, push backward with flow. Push the body by pushing the arm. That only force and flow in one direction. What about force and flow in the other five (six) directions?

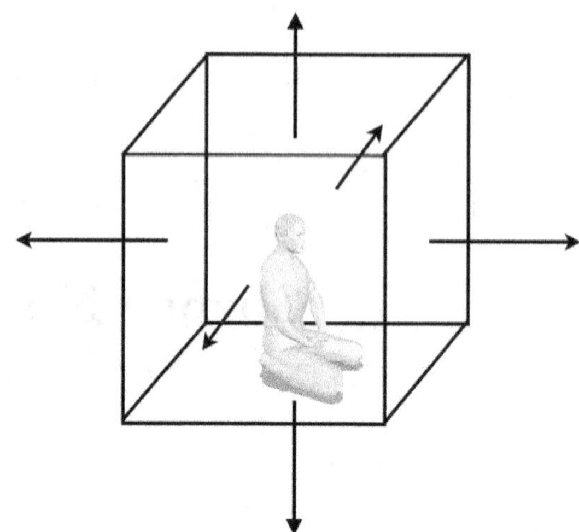

If you fill out a matrix, I would call it the Matrix of Six Directions, this is what it looks like.

	forward	back	right	left	up	down
		XXX		XXX		

You have only pushed a person back. Three different ways, but still only back.

Consider the following techniques

Catch the hand with roll back and pull back and down.

Or, catch the arm and execute a front kick to the groin with the front foot. (Not the back foot, too easy to see that coming).

Or, just put a little snap into the technique, you might have to turn the hips more than is shown in the image, and break the arm.

The Matrix of Six Directions now looks like this.

	forward	back	right	left	up	down
	XXX	XXX	XXX	XXX		

Now, some directions might not work. But you have to explore the matrix for each technique, and for force and flow solutions. Understanding what doesn't work is just as important as understanding what does work.

Chapter Ten
Pole Position/Ward Off

Below are the videos for this section.

Pole Position/Ward Off
https://youtu.be/9Tfwomk5348

WARD OFF

One of the original moves from Tai Chi Chuan, Ward Off has grace, elegance, and a simple and very real function self defense wise.

Step back with the right foot into a back stance as you execute a left vertical palm to protect the face, and a right vertical (down) palm to protect the groin.

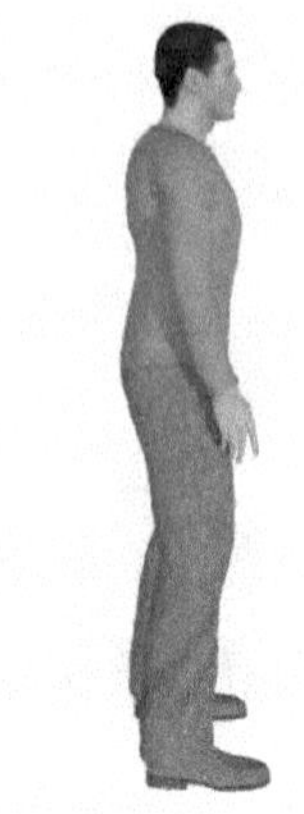

Begin moving forward and turning the waist to the right while bring the left arm up in a horizontal circle, and stroking over the wrist with the right hand.

This last move is sometimes called 'stroking the parrots tail,' or 'stroking the horse's mane.

Move into a front stance as you open the left arm into a half circle and moving the right arm into a position like a low block to the right.

One can use this move as an entry motion for a variety of Tai Chi Chuan moves and techniques.

WARD OFF
PROMISE FIGHTS

When the attacker moves forward with a left punch, the defender must execute a right palm block and get close enough to place his left forearm on the attacker's body.

Start to move forward as you bring the left forearm up to the attacker's body.

Push (you may shuffle forward) and send the Attacker flying.

The technique should be very soft. Yes, you can strike with the left forearm to the body and do damage, but the real technique is to place your arm on the attacker's body so gently that he doesn't perceive the danger, and push.

95

Chapter Eleven
Punch Under

Below are the videos for this section.

9 square diagram punch under
https://youtu.be/2UoCwrMYVOE

PUNCH UNDER

Stand on the center square in a natural stance.

Begin stepping back with the left foot as you bring the left arm out and up and in. Bring the right arm under in a scoop.

Continue stepping back and continue the motion of the hands with the left arm passing behind the right arm.

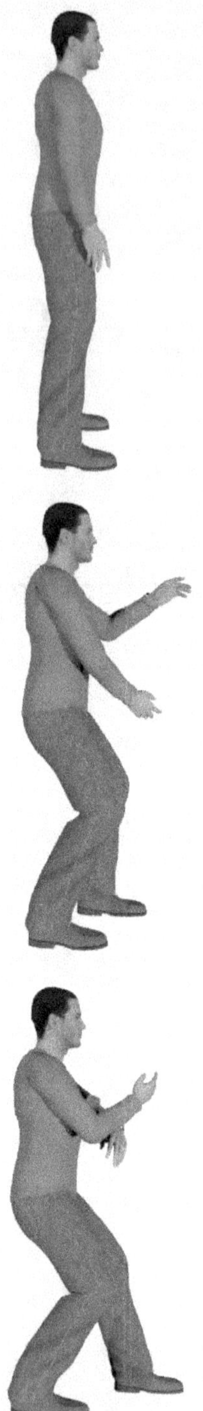

Continue stepping back and pivot the hips to the right into a back stance as you execute a left low block with the palm pointing inward (presenting the palm bone) and a right high block.

Continue the circle of the right arm back and around to the chamber position for a punch. The left arm reverse direction, going up and out from the low block preparing for a cross palm block.

Shift into a front stance, turning the hips to the square position as you execute a right punch under a left palm block.

Pivot into the second move on the square and continue with the form.

PUNCH UNDER
PROMISE FIGHTS

This promise fight addresses the question of the opponent leading off with a kick. the solution is it doesn't matter. Block the kick and start matrixing one or two punches as you wish.

The attacker kicks with the right foot. The defender does the low block/high block sequence from Punch Under.

The attacker follows up with a right punch. The defender executes the second half of Punch Under with a left cross palm and right punch under.

Make sure you explore the possibilities of the attacker punching with the right hand.

On the following pages are some nasty, little things you can do.

After executing the Punch Under promise fight the defender wraps the attackers arm, pushing the back of the hand up towards a wrist lock, and circling the attacker's right elbow, inverting the arm, and pointing towards the ground.

This is a wonderful technique that almost nobody does, in spite of the fact that it is extremely workable.

One can slap the face with the right hand when circling the elbow. This is what we call 'shock and lock. Sometimes the opponent is set and ready and needs a little wake up call. So you punch or slap him in a distracting manner. His attention goes away from resistance and you can then make the technique work.

Once the arm is circled you should point at the ground with one finger. I have been told various ways of making this work. For instance, in Aikido they say chop the hand down the center of the body, then point the hand at the ground. And there are others. I use the index finger pointing at the ground for the simple reason that it is intention that makes the technique work, and simply pointing unleashes intention.

If you end up muscling the fellow then you are doing it wrong. Do it again and avoid setting up resistance in your partner.

The strongest thing in the universe is intention. The easiest way to make intention work is to create emptiness. First in the mind, then in the body.

Another clever addition is to do the Punch Under promise fight, then simply strike in with the left forearm on the elbow, and pull back on the wrist with the right forearm. This should break the arm.

If the arm doesn't break, or if you are just feeling a little mean, chop the neck with the left hand. You should make sure you twist the hips and align the body to get the most out of this technique.

One can do several things at this point.

On this page I show a simple punch to the body. On the next page, however, we go into takedowns. You should always take your promise fight to the end. Go from the initial block all the way through to a takedown whenever possible. Never leave an opponent standing.

To do this technique you should shuffle forward, behind the opponent with a horse stance. The left arm goes across the neck.

This is called 'splitting.' Splitting is when the top of the body goes one way, and the bottom of the body goes the other way.

You can see there are all sorts of other things you can do. You can even do some of the sequences out of order. So, how can you apply the Matrix of Six Directions to this technique?

	forward	back	right	left	up	down

Chapter Twelve
Matrixing Attacks (part one)

There are six distances you need to concern yourself with:

> weapons
> kicking
> punching
> kneeing
> elbowing
> grappling

Here are some truths for you to consider.

A person will attack you with a weapon. You must learn to shift outside the range of the weapon (or sidestep), and close fast enough to negate the weapon. This manipulation of distance should be accomplished within one technique.

Kicking can happen, but legs are slow enough that, with a bit of hard training, you can see them coming and handle them easily.

Most attacks will come the strong side of the opponent's body. Since only 1 out of 8 people are left handed, or 7 out of 8 people are right handed, the actual statistic is 87.5% of the attacks will come from the right side. Most of these attacks will be with the right hand. Since, in the beginning, a straight line is faster than a circle in covering the distance between two points, you should practice your straight punch until it is faster than a magician's card trick. This means getting rid of time between the start and stop of your technique.

Knees can be quite harmful, one should try to stay at punching distance, or that distance at which one has the advantage and the opponent has the disadvantage.

Elbows can be deadly, but they tend to be easy to train for and to stop. At any rate, once one has closed to kneeing and elbowing they are on their way to a clinch. A good rule of thumb is that distance collapses in a fight, and one should be prepared for clinches, and the resulting grapple and takedown.

One method of understanding a fighter is to analyze him by testing him with a quick motion, and ascertaining whether he is a runner, blocker or charger. This isn't bad for beginners, but to really understand fighting you have to understand the following matrix.

	enter	close	finish
enter	enter/enter	enter/close	enter/finish
close	close/enter	close/close	close/finish
finish	finish/enter	finish/close	finish/finish

The above matrix represents the three stages of a fight, which stages can be understood by analyzing time.

For instance, the first box is 'enter/enter.' This means somebody enters the fight by throwing a punch. If the person backs up, if he runs, then he must enter the fight again.

Or, the second box is 'enter/close.' This means somebody enters the fight and closes to the knee/elbow distance. Once one has entered the 'knee/elbow distance the fight is likely to close to a clinch and takedown.

The third box is 'enter/finish.' This means somebody punches you and the fight is over. The punch is either strong enough to finish you, or he is able to straight from the punch to the takedown.

One should write down the nine boxes and analyze them in order to understand their strengths and weaknesses. This will better enable a person to understand what techniques he should be focusing on in his training.

You must cultivate yourself as not a runner, blocker or charger, for if you are bound by one mode you will become victim to the other two. Which is to say if you run all the time, when blocking or charging is needed you will be lacking. And the is true for each of the other two modes of fighting.

One must be equally adept for each of the three modes, and this can only be done through understanding the above matrix and working through the potentials each of the nine boxes in the matrix offer.

And, one must do without the need to make a 'pre-motion' to ascertain whether somebody is a type of fighter. You should learn to look and simply 'know' what kind of fighter the other person is.

And, one should never limit oneself to the idea that because a person is one type of fighter or another, he can't do something out of the box and surprising.

Chapter Thirteen
White Snake/Fair Lady

Below are the videos for this section.

White Snake/Fair Lady
https://youtu.be/kOGj8Oy8SpA

WHITE SNAKE/
FAIR LADY

Begin from the natural stance standing in the center square.

Begin stepping back with the right foot as you cover the face with a palm block and the mid section with a left inverted low block.

This is actually called the 'Inverted Pole Position,' as it looks like you are holding a pole straight up and down, with the lower hand 'inverted,' when viewed from the front.

Continue stepping back with the right foot and sink into a back stance as you continue the movement of the arms to execute a right parry and left outward middle block.

I teach this move Tai Chi style. Once the student has it down I show him how to flick the left hand over, keeping the focus solely in the hand.

Pivot slightly to the right. Your body should be held steady. It is not a hard block, but rather just shifting the outward middle block into the inward middle block. When an attacker hits the block, because you are holding the correct position with the body aligned to the planet, it should be like he is running into the planet in the form of your forearm.

When you pivot from out block to in block you will feel your leg filling up with energy. Use that energy to push into the last move. It should feel like a snake uncoiling inside your rear leg.

Shift forward into a front stance as you execute a left high block and a right palm thrust to the chest.

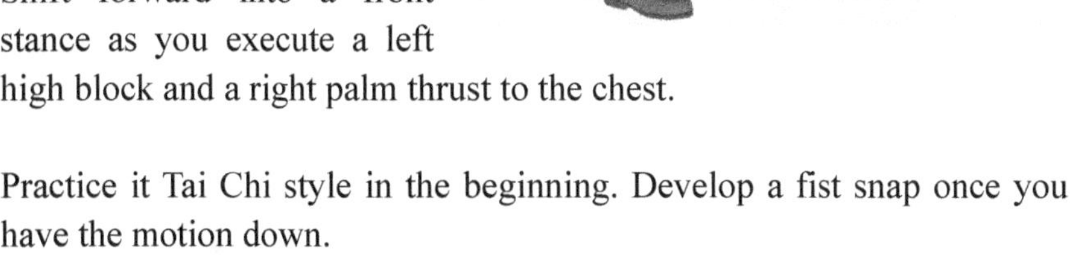

Practice it Tai Chi style in the beginning. Develop a fist snap once you have the motion down.

Pivot into the second move on the Nine Square and continue with the form.

FAIR LADY
PROMISE FIGHTS

Starting from handshake distance apart, the attacker steps back with the left foot and prepares to strike.

The attacker steps forward with the left foot into a front stance as he executes a left middle punch. The defender steps back with the right foot as he executes a palm block with the right hand.

The attacker executes a right middle punch. The defender pivots to the right into a back stance as he executes a left outward block. It is good to strike the biceps.

The attacker executes a left middle punch. The defender pivots to the right changing the outward middle block into an inward middle block. The defender should work on his stance and body alignment so that the defender runs into the block and hurts himself.

The attacker punches to face with the right hand. The defender pivots to the left and shifts into a front stance as he executes 'Fair Lady,' which is a left high block and right palm to the chest.

The final palm can be a 'plant and push,' or a 'pulsing palm.'

You can break this technique into two techniques for beginners, then put it together for the full four strike potential later on.

On the following page we will take a look at some of the potentials that can result from this technique. I like to teach a class showing just the technique this far, then change up the following takedowns over the weeks, always giving the students something new to think about, but without messing up the basic block and counter move.

At the end of the initial technique the defender can grab the attacker's right wrist and shift backward, pulling the attacker forward as he kicks the attacker's left knee or sweeps the attacker's left leg.

Another option is to simply grab the attacker's neck or shoulders and pull him into a knee strike. If the attacker lowers his hand to block the knee the head and neck are open for further manipulations.

After the initial technique is done, have the attacker punch a fifth time with the left hand to the belly. The defender shifts back and parries with the left arm. This turns the attacker so he can be pushed off balance with a right hand to the shoulder. This final move looks a bit like Roll Back, but that is okay. All moves, all postures, are interchangeable. That's basic matrixing.

Another technique, more complex, is shown in the last image on this page. This requires the defender to angulate a bit, shift his position and drive in to shoot his right arm under the attacker's left arm. The defender twines the attacker's arm in a 'figure four' armlock. The arm can then be broken easily, or the defender simply taken down.

Chapter Fourteen
Six Distances

There are six distances one should familiarize themselves with. These distances are: weapons, kick, punch, knee, elbow, grappling.

Each of these weapons has unique properties. Weapons, for instance, can be rematrixed with the various weapons.

I usually only work with four distances: kick, punch, knee, elbow. It is easy enough to understand that you are going to have to move forward to meet a weapon, or away. And, I teach different courses, specifically Monkey Boxing and Kenjutsu, to work with weapons.

Below is a matrix illustrating the four weapons I focus on.

	kick	punch	knee	elbow
kick	K/K	K/P	K/KN	K/E
punch	P/K	P/P	P/KN	P/E
knee	KN/K	KN/P	KN/KN	KN/E
elbow	E/K	E/P	E/KN	E/E

Obviously, one is going to have to consider such simple but significant items such as: There are two sides. For instance, a right kick or a left kick.

There are two directions. for instance, a right punch can be opened or closed.

Each weapon requires specific and different angulations, hip movements, weight shifts, and so on

In the open hands portion of Monkey Boxing I use a matrix like this:

This graph shows that one must become acquainted with fighting from kick to kick distance, kick to punch distance, kick to knee distance, and so on through all the distances.

Now, you can see that the simplicity of Nine Square Diagram Boxing is opening up into unimaginable complexities...all based on more simplicities. So how much of these matrixes do you have to do? Do you have to go through the complete Matrix of Directions, the Matrix of Distances. Do you have to explore all the distance to distances in the above Monkey Boxing graph?

You need to do a little work, but just to the point where you grasp the concept. Look, this is very intuitive stuff. Sure, there may be a guy out in Poughkeepsie who has to go through every technique in every matrix to get to the truth. But most people just have to do a few, play around with the matrix, and then let it settle in their minds.

Here is the secret: this stuff is so logical that the mind likes it. The mind will blink a bit, then simply absorb it. Without fanfare or extra thought or significant attempts at mental obfuscation.

The mind LOVES what is simple and logical.

So the final question is this: What other Promise Fights can you find? Work both sides of the body, explore punches, kicks, knees and elbows. consider breaks and throws. Guaranteed there are about a dozen more things you can do. Can you find them?

Eventually, of course, if practice long enough you will find them all. But using matrixing you should be able to find them all in a short period of time. Using a matrix makes you learn faster, and that is the secret of why I say I can get people to black belt in a matter of months.

By the way, I won't be breaking down each and every technique of the Nine Square Diagram like this. You are expected to do that yourself. Aside from the sheer amount of work, and a resulting book of a thousand pages, it is always better for the student to discover for himself or herself.

Do not memorize, learn to think, to analyze. Guaranteed, you will become intuitive ten times faster if you learn through this method.

CAUTION!

You will finds lots of places where a technique just simply doesn't work. At these points you should remember that it is not important to always be right…it is important to see what is wrong. The most important thing in the martial arts is to learn. It is difficult to learn if you can't see nor acknowledge your mistakes…in this case, the 'mistakes,' or things that simply don't work in an art.

You will learn less from doing something right a thousand times, than simply seeing what doesn't work once.

Chapter Fifteen
White Crane

Below are the videos for this section.

White Crane
https://youtu.be/4jTON6cRmh4

CRANE

Start from the natural stance on the center square.

Begin stepping back with the right foot as you bring the right hand out and around in a palm block The left hand goes in front of the lower body in an inverted low block.

Sink onto the right leg as you execute a left front snap kick and a left outward middle block. The right hand is in the parry position.

Show the form Tai Chi style at first. When the student has it down, execute snap in the kick and block.

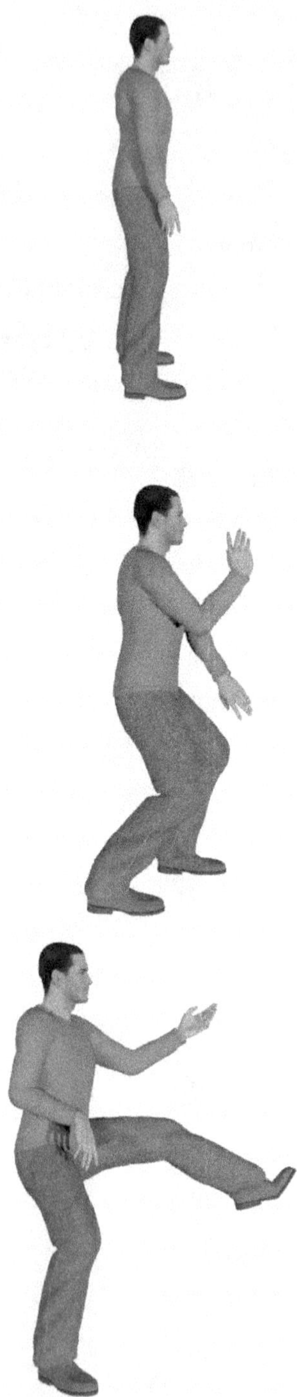

Step forward with the left foot into a front stance as you execute a right elbow to the left palm.

Pivot to the right and circle the arms out to continue the form.

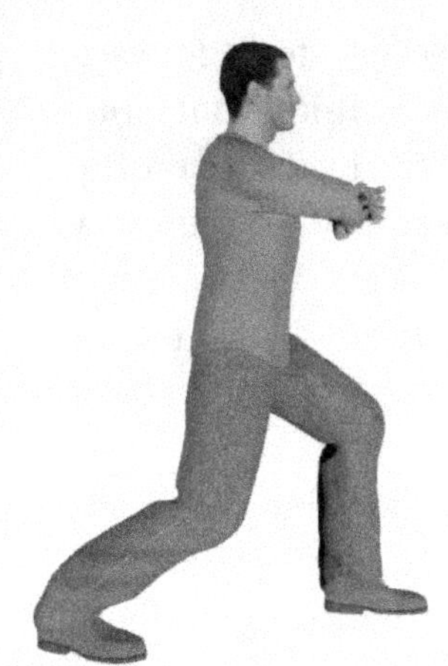

The attacker steps forward with the right foot and punches. The defender simultaneously executes a left snap kick to the groin and a left outward block to the biceps,

The defender grabs the back of the attacker's head and pulls him into a right elbow strike.

The defender pushes the attacker's right arm up and around as he pushes down on the attacker's neck with the right arm.

This is actually a classical technique from Kang Duk Won. Of course, most techniques can be found in most systems.

I used to kick fast and strike the belly with the foot.

You can do a simple outward middle block, but I always like laying the back of the hand, or the knuckles, on the attacker's biceps. Lot of pain can be generated when you focus your counters.

Chapter Sixteen
Single Whip

Below are the videos for this section.

Single Whip
https://youtu.be/XGzIggxcYlc

SINGLE WHIP

Start from the natural stance on the center square.

Begin stepping back with the right foot as you bring the left hand out and up. The right hand should scoop across the body.

Continue stepping back as you continue the motions of the arms, crossing them in front fo the body as the left hand goes down and the right hand goes up.

This form begins much like Punch Under.

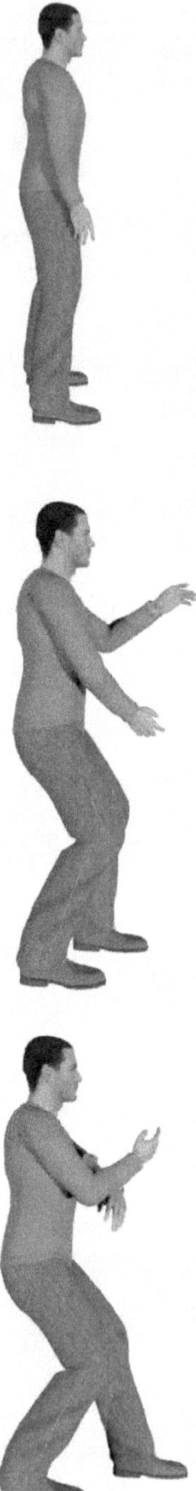

Sink into a back stance as you execute a left low block (palm turned in so the fingers point across the body and the palm bone does the block) and a right high block.

Continue circling the arms so that the left had executes a cross palm block and the right hand scoops across the front of the body. The hips should turn slightly to the left with this motion.

Continue the circling motion of the arms, the left hand circling to the palm position and the right arm going through the high block position.

Continue the circling of the motion to a left small circle of the wrist and a right single whip. We sometimes call this hand configuration the 'little beak,' or the 'little fist.' You should turn the hips slightly to the right to assume a back stance.

Shift the weight forward into a front stance as you finish the circle of the wrist and push the left palm forward.

If you look at this form carefully you will realize that there is a'slap grab' inherent in the motion.

The attacker executes a right kick. The defender moves the right leg back into a back stance as he executes a left low block and a right high block.

The attacker sets the right leg down and executes a right punch. The defender brings the left hand up in a palm block (slap). The right hand circles back and around and across the body in a scooping motion.

The defender brings the right hand up and grabs the attacker's right wrist.

Obviously, one can work this technique with the attacker punching with either hand.

The defender pulls the attacker's wrist with his right hand and turns the hips slightly to the right as he pulse punches to the attacker's mid-section.

Obviously, one can apply a palm to the elbow and do an armbar/elbow roll.

If the attacker is punching with the other hand it is fun to look for take downs and ways to unbalance the attacker.

One may have realized, by now, that there are incredible numbers of techniques that can be created for the Nine Square. The first five I showed you in this book are the ones I prefer. the last three are also very good, but I work on the first five for the most part.

I have actually done a complete breakdown of Nine Square techniques, as taken from Tai Chi Chuan. I filmed nearly 200 segments going into the complete matrix of Tai Chi techniques. Eventually these will be released, and they will show the research I did, and hopefully give others ideas on how to create the martial arts.

Chapter Seventeen
Matrixing Attacks (Part Two)

I have configured large matrixes with the data in this chapter, but one needs to start with a simple matrix. Learn the simple, and you will be able to understand, and even create matrixes for, the larger potentials.

Here is a simple matrix of attacks.

In this matrix we are only going to consider the punching distance.

Kicks are too easy to see.

Weapons are even further away, which gives more time to analyze the attack and alter your defense accordingly.

If you become adept at punching you can keep the attacker at punching distance, and avoid kneeing, elbowing and the resultant grappling distances.

	right	left
right	right/right	right/left
left	left/right	left/left

What this means is that you are going to have to deal with one of the following attacks.

right/right	right/left
left/right	left/left

In a fight you don't assume there will only be one attack. You don't assume there will be three attacks, because:

1 a person punches with the right and you block.

2 then punches with the left and you block.

3 if he punches again you don't assume it is a third punch, you forget about the first punch as being number one, and make the second punch number one in your mind, and the third punch is number two.

4 if he punches again you don't assume it is a fourth punch, you forget about the second punch as being number two, and make the third punch number one in your mind, and the fourth punch is number two.

5 And so on. Thus, no matter how many punches a fellow throws at you, you absorb the attacks, maybe backing up a little, and when he has become either exhausted or predictable, you finish the fight.

The point of the above section is that you never leave the mode of handling two punches.

Now, technically, there should never be a second punch launched at you. You should knock the fellow out, or manipulate him to a finish, before there is a second punch, and, if you are good, before there is a first punch.

But, for training purposes we will assume two punches. And, with matrixing we can analyze the situation as follows.

	open	close
open	open/open	open/close
close	close/open	close/close

When a person throws a right punch, if you push (block) the attack across the body, then you have 'closed' the punch.

When a person throws a right punch, if you push (block) the attack away, which is to say exposing his body, then you have 'open' the punch.

Thus, there are four combinations you have to deal with.

open/open	open/close
close/open	close/close

Now, here comes something you should understand about this system: this system is based on handling the four attacks. It may seem a little random at times, but that is just to take into account a few variations and 'what ifs,' and to make sure the system doesn't become 'one dimensional.'

Do this system and you will understand the core of the martial arts. When you study other martial arts you must always keep this system foremost in your mind, and you must keep it pure. If you add or subtract from it you risk destroying the logic that I have put into it.

Chapter Eighteen
Horn Punch

Below are the videos for this section.

9 square diagram horn punch
https://youtu.be/mvdYUZL0ssg

HORN PUNCH

Begin stepping back as you bring both arms out and down, then upwards crossed.

Snap both fists outward in inverted outward blocks.

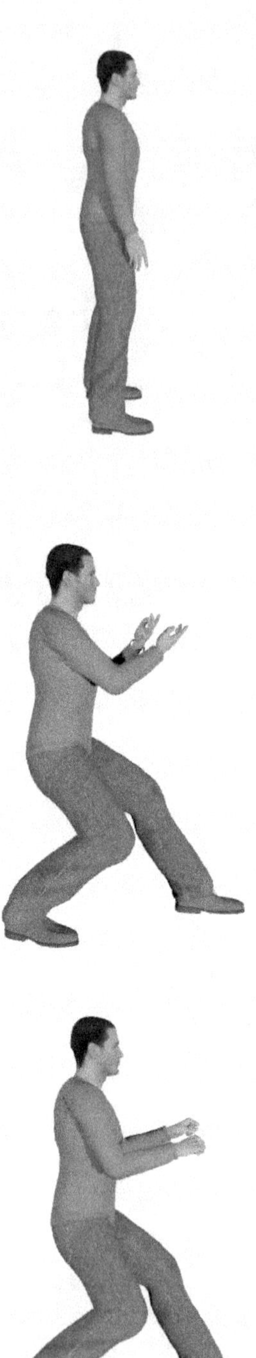

Bring the arms slightly upward and inward then downward to cross.

Bring the arms all the way down and circle outward as you begin shifting foreward.

Shift into a front stance as you execute double horn punches.

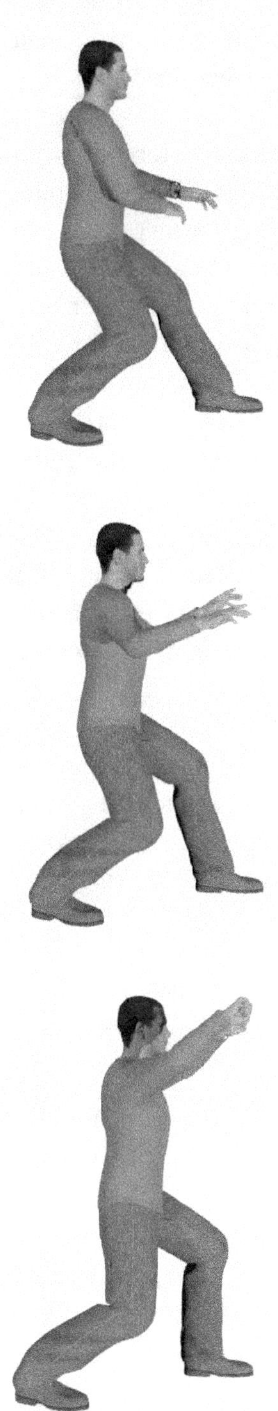

Start facing each other hand shake distance apart.

Attacker steps forward with the right foot and raises both hands to push (grab) the defender's chest. the defender steps back with the left foot into a back stance as he brings both arms up between the attacker's arms and pushes them out and grabs the wrists

The defender pulls the Attacker off balance as he executes a right kick to the groin.

The follow ups are many. A punch or two to the chest. Pulling one wrist and striking with the elbow. Striking with the knee.

A couple of other potentials for this form are on the next page.

If the attacker is shorter, or the arms come in at a lower angle, the defender can separate the push by stepping back with the right foot and executing a double parry.

The defender can simply shuffle forward and hug (break) the neck, execute a choke hold, and so on.

One can easily use a 'Slap Grab' technique to turn the attacker sideways.

The Horn Punch Form is also the form in which I teach crossed wrist high blocks, low and high, for taking away weapons, stopping kicks, and moving into jointlocks or throws.

The attacker steps forward with the right foot and pushes to the chest with both arms. The defender steps back as he separates the attacker's arms.

The attacker shuffles forward into a front stance as he executes double horn punches to the temples.

One can gouge the eyes, stick thumbs in the neck, go into a choke, all manner of things.

Chapter Nineteen
Rolling Fist
(also called Punch Over)

Below are the videos for this section.

9 square diagram punch over
https://youtu.be/hbDK_wv2xK0

ROLLING FIST

Start in the natural stance.

Begin stepping back with the right foot as you begin circling the left hand inward and upward, and the right hand o ver and downward.

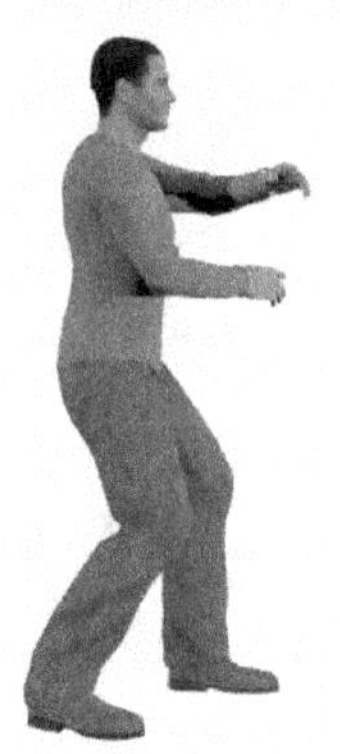

Continue stepping back as you continue the circle of the arms. The left hand goes through the high block position and the right hand goes through the low block position.

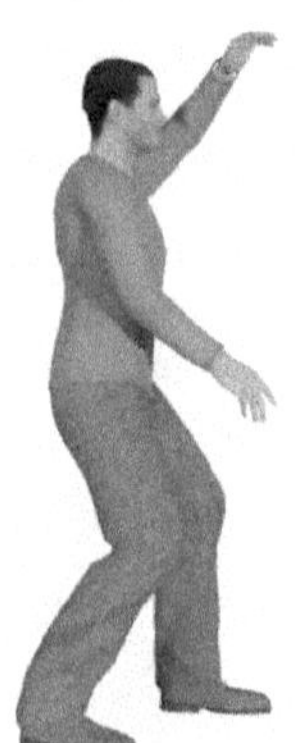

Continue stepping back as you continue circling the arms.

Continue stepping back as you continue circling the arms, bringing the right arm to a palm block covering the face, and the left arm to an inverted low block.

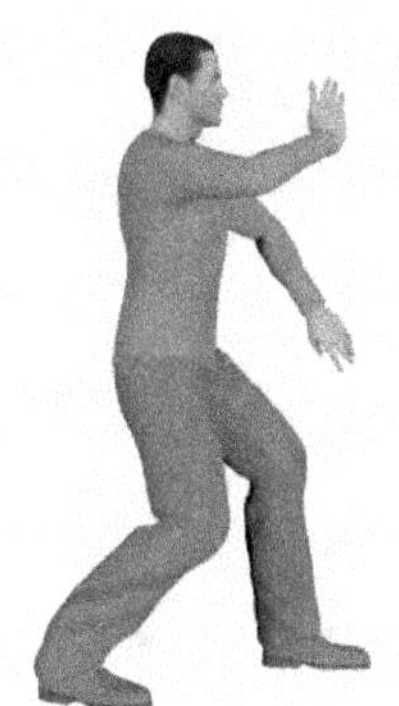

Sink into a back stance as you snap the left fist over the right palm.

Pivot to the right and continue the form.

ROLLING FIST
PROMISE FIGHTS

I do drills instead of promise fights for the Rolling Fist. Here is a breakdown of the first Rolling Fist Drill, which I call 'Rolling the Wall.' I call it Rolling the Wall because the student is supposed to hit a pad on a wall, or a bag, or some other semi-resisting object.

Strike a bag using these four strikes. No circles or anything, simply jackhammer the bag with straight back and forth strikes in any order. The student will find his own favorite sequences.

After the 'Straight Strike,' presented on the last page, the student moves to the 'Half Circle.'

Alternate these two strikes. You will have to do a 'half circle' motion. do not cock, just circle the hands.

The left strikes low the right hand covers high. Then the left hand strikes high and the right hand strikes low.

Then do this drill with the rear hand.

Then do this drill with the right foot forward and the left foot back.

Then do the drill while taking a triangle step to the side. This will aid the student in understanding how to step off the line of attack.

After doing the 'Straight Strike,' and the Half Roll,' the student is ready to do the 'Full Roll.'

Roll the right hand in a full circle. The blocking hand should roll in a circle, too.

Practice rolling forward.
Practice rolling backward.
Practice with the left hand.
Practice with the left foot back and the right foot forward.

Finally, mix the full circle of the fist with the half circle of the presented presented on the last page.

After doing the Straight Strike, the Half Roll, and the Roll, the student is ready for the 'Roll and a Half.'

When you are adept at the straight strike, the half roll, the full roll, then attempt the roll and a half.

In the 'Roll and a Half' drill you simply do a full circle, and continue the roll so that the other hand strikes.

Do on both sides.
Do forwards and backwards.
Do on a triangle step.

Finally, begin mixing the Roll and a Half with the first three strikes.

I usually do these strikes on a heavy bag, and every strike is supposed to knock the bag bag severely.

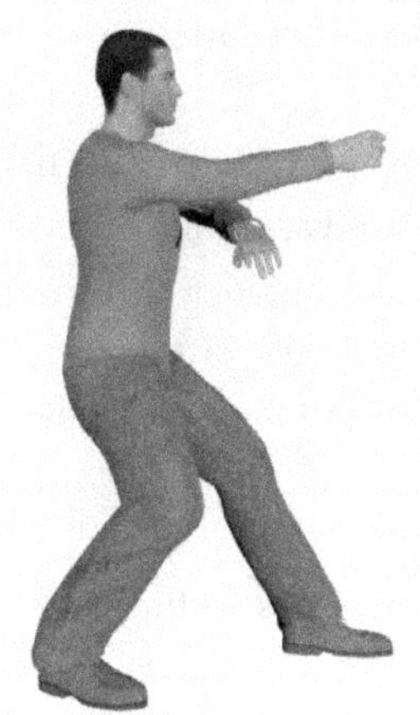

ROLLING FIST
TWO MAN DRILL

This is a very simple drill with MANY variations.

Attacker punches to the face, defender high blocks with the same side arm.

Attacker punches to the body with the other hand. The defender rolls his right hand over and down on the attacker's arm.

The attack and defender change roles, the attacker becoming the defender and the defender becoming the attacker.

The defender rolls his left fist over his own block to touch the attacker in the chest.

This drill can be done in place, while advancing or retreating, moving side to side, and so on.

One can make this incredibly complex by adding attacks, varying defenses, and so on. Best to stick to the simple basics in the beginning, however.

Chapter Twenty
Slap Grab

Below are the videos for this section.

9 square diagram slap grab
https://youtu.be/SUukkgeFFDg

SLAP GRAB

Start from the natural stance in the center square.

Begin stepping back with the right foot. As you step bring the left hand out and around and point the fingers down. The right hand should start circling outward.

Sink into a back stance as you execute a snapping downward palm and a right palm block. the right palm block is the slap, the next move is the grab.

Search for circles to make the move faster.

Bring the right hand back as you circle the left hand into an outward grabbing block.

Bring the left hand back as if pulling as you strike with the right vertical punch.

Bring the right hand under as if scooping. the left hand executes a left palm block (slap).

Turn the hips slightly into each move.

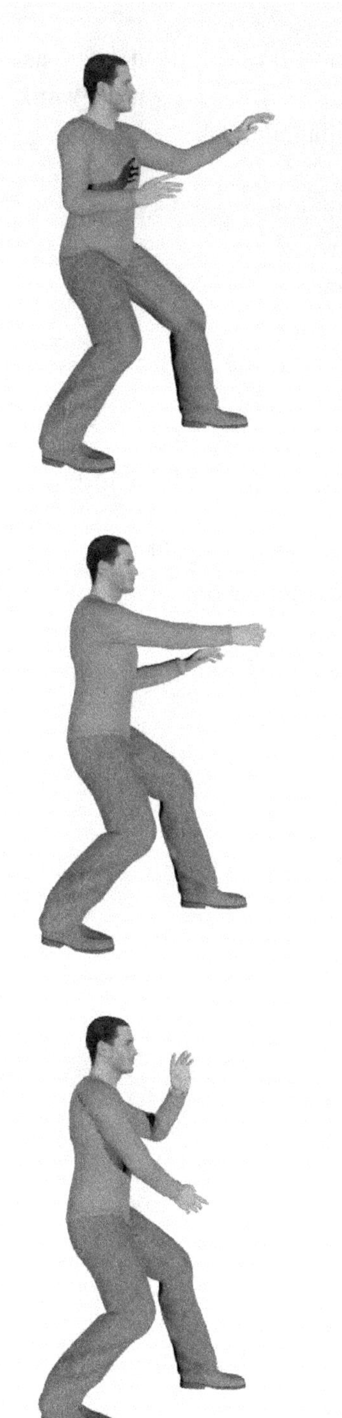

Bring the left hand back as you execute a right outward grabbing block.

Bring the right hand back as you execute a left vertical punch.

Pivot to the right and repeat the sequence.

Continue through the form.

This form should sink you into the ground.

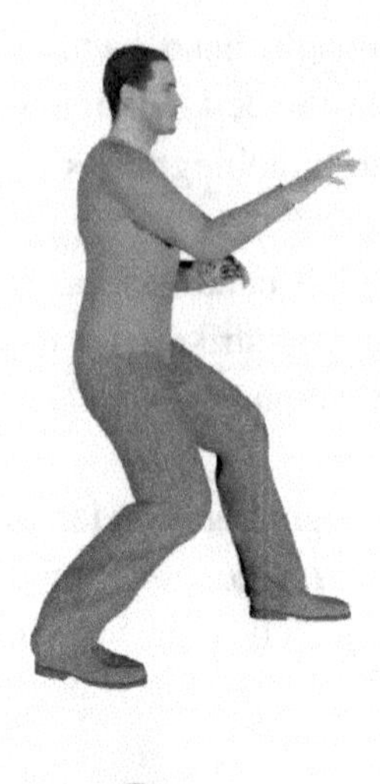

SLAP GRAB
PROMISE FIGHTS

'The Perfect Technique'

This is the Perfect Technique. It is applicable to either fist, either side of any fist.

Which is to say it can be used for any combination of punches: right/left, right/right, left/right and left/left.

The attacker punches with the right hand. The defender slaps with the left hand.

The defender scoops the right hand under and over to grab the attacker's right wrist.

The second half of this technique is on the following page.

One can expand the technique to fit the form quite easily. Simply use the palm down block for a foot, then slide into the perfect technique.

There will be more information on this perfect technique in a few pages.

The attacker punches with the left hand. The defender slaps the attack with his right hand.

The defender scoops his left hand under and over to grab the attacker's left wrist.

The defender holds the wrist and pulls slightly as he punches with the right hand.

This sequence of images shows a defender closing both hands. Obviously, as will be gone over, one can open both hands, or close and open, or open and close.

One can drill the technique, throwing a dozen or so punches, then the partners shift roles, the attacker becoming the defender, and the defender becoming the attacker.

Or, they can trade off after every two punches.

Chapter Twenty-One
Matrixing Attacks (Part Three)

'The Perfect Technique'

In Nine Square Diagram Boxing you have experienced a logical breakdown of art that will effect you in many ways, and all arts in many ways. I do like to encourage people to work on one speecific technique endlessly, as it is the perfect technique, which is to say it works on the right side or the left side, opening or closing.

One of my severe breakthroughs was when I discovered that the art is not any of the techniques or sequences of techniques I had learned.

One must practice techniques, and by that I mean at least a small variety of techniques, to increase speed, ability, understanding, intuition, and so on. However, the first technique of the martial arts, and the one upon which ALL other techniques should be based upon is the simple slap.

If a fly is buzzing front of you you don't launch a block, or execute fancy footwork to evade the predator. Instead, you simply slap it.

Now, in this universe there is only force and flow. Which is to say there are objects, and the directions objects take when homing in on you.

One can do one of two things: evade or block. No matter the art, any technique can be broken down to these two possibilities.

Step out of the way (flow it), or deal with the object through the use of force…bat it (block it).

One should, actually, do both. One should step out of the way and…slap it.

To understand this one should understand that one raises the hand to slap, then closes the hand to grab (guide, manipulate, etc.), and finally to block.

Thus, blocking is actually third in the sequence of possible things to do when under attack.

So the perfect technique involves a slight shift to take one off the line of attack, then slapping the attack, then grabbing.

In doing this attack one handles entering the fight, and by using the 'slap/grab' properly, translates all the way into a finish.

Mind you, one can use a variety of other possibles. One can inject knees and elbows, translate other throws, and so on, but the Perfect Technique, the one that handles virtually every possible attack right to the ground and an unconscious or broken opponent, goes like this.

kick   close or open with a slight shift and low slap
punch   close or open with a slap and grab
                takedown

The matrix (in list form) for 'The Perfect Technique' is on the following page.

Chapter Twenty-Two
Freestyle

Below are the videos for this section.

9 square push hands
https://youtu.be/5R8VD300wac

9 square diagram push hands end
https://youtu.be/rCy8wyR2WYs

nine square lop sau extra
https://youtu.be/OB1MABgL1fo

push hands extra
https://youtu.be/Nxj_Rx3lf1o

FREESTYLE

People always think Karate is about fighting. It's not.

It's about not fighting. It's about living a good life, getting along with people, being healthy through old age, helping people, and so on.

But, since most people can't be convinced that what I'm saying is true without a few decades of being punched in the head, let me give you my method for teaching freestyle. It is a sure fire method, doesn't include bruises (at least too much), and totally changes the way a person looks are the world.

Consider the following list.

white belt	see/think/react
green belt	see/react
brown belt	react
black belt	act
master	act before

The point behind this list is that martial arts grows intuition. You stop reacting to the world, and start acting…and even acting before.

My freestyle drills mirror this, although there is some liquidity between when a person does a drill and when he gets the result.

There is a lot of liquidity in when I teach which drill. Karate is so simple, the martial arts are so simple, I teach what I feel like when I feel like it.

white belt	see/think/react	rhythmic freestyle
green belt	see/react	two strike rhythmic freestyle
brown belt	react	one way freestyle
black belt	act	lop sau
master	act before	

I also use other drills, depending upon when the student is ready for them. Specifically, I use Sticky Hands (Wing chun Kung Fu) and Push Hands (Tai Chi Chuan).

On the following pages are a breakdown of the various types of freestyle, but I want to caution you first.

When I learned to freestyle in the martial arts the instructor put my hands up and told me not to let him hit me. That was my only instruction. He then beat the crap out of me.

But who would want to be beaten and confused and convinced that somebody else is better? I turned out to be one of the ones that liked pain and hard work outs, but it still took me years to overcome that lesson.

Would you like and trust somebody who beat you up and called it a lesson?

So when you learn freestyle, or better, when you teach freestyle, specifically the drills I show you here, remember one thing: people don't want to keep doing things that hurt. Show them how to have fun. Let the desire to learn hurt later. Guaranteed, if you do the techniques right, the freestyle drills don't have to be brutal.

I re-emphasize:

Nobody wants to go to a school just to get beat up.
They go to school to learn.
And the best way to learn is to have fun.
Period.

Following is the sequence of drills that I use to teach people how to fight. It is the fastest and most efficient method in the world, and it teaches people how to think inside of combat, and to become intuitive in their martial arts and life.

RHYTHMIC FREESTYLE

Rhythmic Freestyle is fun. The sooner I get a person into it, the better it is for that person. It changes their ideas and expectations rather quickly.

Student One strikes and student two blocks. Then Student Two strikes and Student One blocks. And they keep going, alternating striking and block.

THEY DO THIS SLOWLY! The essence of this drill is not to beat somebody up, it is to teach. thus, when Student One strikes, he is not trying to beat Student Two, but to teach him to respond.

If you strike fast the student is confused. If you strike too hard, the student is hurt. Who would want to continue learning if all they got was confused and hurt?

But if you strike slowly, the student can figure it out. It only takes a couple of minutes for this drill to become fun and start the intuition process.

Here are some rules.

Take a step when you strike, take a step when you block. Don't take two steps to your partner's one, that's not what is going to happen in a fight. People don't suddenly whirl their arms faster than a magician and confuse the other person…the other person is moving, too, and you have to learn to deal with his motion. He is NOT a sitting duck, like some people would falsely have you believe.

Don't move faster than you, or your partner, knows. That is a sure path to injury. In fact, I say this very succinctly in something I call 'The Injury Formula.'

Speed + Ignorance = Injury

Don't think that what you are doing is wrong, even if it looks like the biggest mistake in the world. It is what you did, and what you did in a real situation. Go through it. Figure it out. Time spent looking at 'mistakes' is some of the best instruction you will have in the world.
It is okay to do this with weapons, even from the first lesson. Just go slow and let your partner figure it out. DON'T USE REAL WEAPONS!

Concentrate on strikes, save takedowns for a future time. When strikes are mastered then takedowns can be taught and inserted, but only if you leave your partner a way out. When you are doing Rhythmic Freestyle with takedowns and locks and such we called it 'Flowstyle.'

TWO ON ONE RHYTHMIC FREESTYLE

When you have an uneven number of people in class you can have two attack one. Make sure you do the drill slowly.

Student One is in the center. Student Two strikes Student One. Student One blocks and counters…and Student Two does not block. Student three strikes Student One. Student One blocks and counters…and Student Three does not block.

Students Two and Three continue to alternate strikes, and Student One blocks and counters.

You can only take one step when you strike, and one step when you block.

This drill is much like the previous Rhythmic Freestyle drill, the real difference is going to be that Student One, the student in the center, is going to find himself trapped between two attackers. He must learn not to let himself get positioned between two people, but to work them so they get in each other's way.

I often tell students, 'don't be the meat, be the bread.' (Don't be between, get one of them between…)

Again, weapons are fine, even right from the get go.

And, if a student finds himself in a bad position (inside the 'sandwich,' he should not take two steps or otherwise escape. He must figure out a way to deal with the situation so that he gets out logically.

TWO STRIKE RHYTHMIC FREESTYLE

This drill is the same as Rhythmic Freestyle, except the attacker strikes twice, and the defender blocks twice. Then the defender becomes the attacker and strikes twice, and the attacker becomes the defender and blocks twice. One step per block or strike.

Move slowly. Remember that you are not fighting, but teaching.

ONE WAY RHYTHMIC FREESTYLE

The Attacker strikes three times, taking a step forward each strike. The Defender blocks each strike, and he may step back once on each strike.

Do not slant off to the side, keep the drill going forward and back.

This drill may be done faster, as previous drills should have prepared the student for reality.

If one of the students isn't accomplished, the drill should be done at a speed which will accommodate the slower student.

The previous drills are strictly learning, no fighting allowed. This drill, however, is the last step before actual fighting (freestyle). It is okay to push the students a little, as long as you don't overwhelm them.

If they have learned the previous drills they should have much trouble. If they do, move them back to the earlier drills.

Time of learning is not important. These drills are so quick they are light years ahead of the normal ways of teaching people how to fight.

FREESTYLE

Light contact on the body. No facial contact.

Your purpose is to learn how to fight, not beat people up, not to render fellow students incapable of continuing. Your purpose is to learn how to fight, not beat people up, not to hand out pain and so discourage other students from continuing.

If you wish to delve into pain, I always tell people to find a partner of like mind and simply do the techniques harder and harder. Make sure your partner can keep up with you (and you him) and that both of you can quell the pain.

If it starts to hurt too much, back off, work a bit, then start increasing impact again and slower.

LOP SAU

Lop Sau means rolling fists. The one exercise I do which elevates all freestyle in my art, and elevates the student to high levels, is Lop Sau. There are only six techniques in Lop Sau. Once a student has learned them his speed of freestyle becomes incredible. At this point I show how to insert the Monkey Boxing Grab Arts into the drill, slick tricks to watch out for, and so on.

The six pieces of Lop Sau are:

> Front punch
> Front hook
> Back hook
> Front kick
> Changing sides
> Changing with a kick

You will find that these six techniques, and their blocks, comprise virtually all the realistic striking arts.

1ST TECHNIQUE IN LOP SAU
ROLLING THE FIST

Partners face each other at handshake distance, each with the same leg forward.

Partner A strikes with a front hand back fist to the face.

Partner B catches the back fist with his rear hand palm block.

When attacking move into a front stance and turn the waist along the plane of the feet.

When defending move into a back stance with the hips square to your opponent.

The back of the fist should slap into the palm like a ball into a glove.

The back fist simulates a jab.

2ND TECHNIQUE IN LOP SAU
FRONT HAND HOOK PUNCH

Instead of striking with a back fist, partner A strikes with a front hand hook to the face.

Partner B executes a back hand high block.

Partner B punches to the mid-section with the front hand.

Partner A utilizes a 'dangling forearm' block.

Partner A rolls back into the circling fist of the first technique.

The drill is based on the constant circling of the fists. Any deviation is followed by a return to the first technique of the drill.

3RD TECHNIQUE IN LOP SAU
REAR HAND HOOK PUNCH

After the first technique is executed, Partner A doesn't move back, but rather executes a rear hand hook to the face.

Partner B executes a front hand high block.

Partner B punches to the mid-section with the rear hand.

Partner A executes a front hand 'dangling forearm' block.

Partner A continues the circle of the dangling forearm into the first technique of the drill.

4TH TECHNIQUE IN LOP SAU
SLAPPING THE FRONT KICK

Instead of striking with the initial
back fist, Partner B executes a kick to
the groin area.

Partner A slaps the ankle outward
with the front hand.

Partner A circles the slap into the first
technique of the drill.

You begin training this drill slowly,
adding pieces slowly, and the speed
of the blocks and strikes begins to
increase.

In a very short time, maybe an hour
or two, the partners are moving with
blinding speed and never miss a block.

5TH TECHNIQUE IN LOP SAU
CHANGING SIDES

Instead of catching the back fist, partner A hooks the inside of partner B's arm and pulls. He should be stepping back with the front foot as he pulls, but only to the depth of his rear foot.

Partner A steps forward with the back foot and strikes with the new front hand.

If partner B has picked up on the change, and changed with the attack, he will catch the back fist with his palm.

If partner B doesn't change a big hole in his defense opens up and Partner A will touch Partner B on the face with his back fist to show it.

It will become apparent quickly that if either partner misses a block, is late, or deviates from the pattern, a hole in his defenses will result.

6TH TECHNIQUE IN LOP SAU
CHANGING WITH A KICK

As in the last technique Partner A executes a hooking pull with his front hand as he changes. Instead of striking with a backfist, however, he will execute a kick with his new front leg.

Partner B should change with partner A and slap the attacking foot on the inside ankle with his new front hand.

Partner B should return to the first technique of the drill.

Chapter Twenty-Three
Beyond Basic-Basics

Below are the videos for this section.

9 square diagram Q and A
https://youtu.be/BAqfaGoJwFY

BEYOND BASIC-BASICS

The study of Basics isn't adequate, and doesn't lead to the True Art.

The Study of Basic-Basics is adequate, and will lead to the True Art.

But what is beyond the Basics-Basics? By this I mean…what abilities will you get by focusing on the Basic-Basics?

THE THREE TYPES OF POWER

Studying the Basic-Basics will reveal certain concepts that are crucial to the True Art.

For instance, the Three Types of Power are: Sinking, Rotating and Thrusting.

Sinking Power merely pertains to Grounding, to sinking the weight while striking, blocking, etc.

Rotating Power refers to turning the hips into the strike or block.

Thrusting Power refers to moving your body forward so that all your weight is utilized in your technique.

To understand these concepts merely look to punching.

If you thrust the body towards the opponent, you punch with the whole body weight.

If you turn the hips into the strike (block, kick), you will also commit the entire body weight to the strike.

If you sink the body weight you better connect to the earth, and the power of your strike will reveal this.

And I should make three points here.

First, punching is not 'how hard you can strike. To believe that is sheer dumbness, and it derails all attempts to find the True Art.

Punching is how much weight you can put on the frame of another.

Speed can increase weight, and is not a bad thing.

But if you work on increasing muscles as necessary to a punch then you are going against the first Basic-Basic of 'Relaxing.'

Second, the case of 'Sinking' you are not introducing weight, so what the heck is going on?

What is going on is you are learning to strike with energy.

Three, when you block you should not focus on introducing weight (except in the beginning, when you are young and 'inexperienced.'

What you should be doing is learning how to assume a posture just before an opponent strikes you so that, your posture being connected to planet earth through stance, and having proper body alignment, he literally 'runs into the planet.'

THE FOURTH POWER

You must learn to CBM the three powers. Which is to say you must examine each stance, each technique, so as to understand what percentage of sinking you are using, what percentage of hip rotation, and what percentage of thrusting.

Each stance is a mix of the Three Powers, and you must have the correct amount of each, appropriate to what you are doing.

If you do this you will discover a Fourth Power. This is the Power of 'Chi.' Which is to say that the energy you have been practicing making, by breathing to the tan tien and CBMing and body and so on, will become manifest.

You will find that your body is capable of much more power than you ever imagined.

And, here is an important factor that you will learn, and which you should probably practice from the beginning: *Less means more!*

The easier you strike a person, the less power you use when striking a person (or blocking or kicking), the more power you will manifest, the more effect you will have on that other person.

I first discovered this, after about twenty years of training, when I struck a person in freestyle and missed. I simply pulled my punch, stopped short by a good two inches, and my partner stood up and started reeling and holding his chin. He swore I had hit him. But I hadn't. I had simply used good control, and less became more.

These days I am extremely careful not to relax too much, as that is when people get hurt.

FORCE VS FLOW

The Martial Arts are a study of force and flow. Unfortunately, nobody really understands Force and Flow.

Force is when two bodies collide. Flow is when two bodies…miss.

Thus, as you progress from the hard to the soft, through the techniques I have listed here, and as you learn to appreciate ever finer tolerances of distances, you will make the natural progression from raging tiger to wily dragon.

UNBALANCING PEOPLE

As I grew in power I found that I could unbalance people simply by moving towards them, or away. It was like my body was a force of nature and they were sucked into the effect.

AFFECTING PEOPLE'S MINDS

I would say things and watch people absorb and change. I am curious as to where this ability would lead, should I have another 50 years or so to practice it. Fortunately, however, since I probably don't have 50+ years, you can prove it for me. Follow the advices and training methods in this book and you will shortly achieve the abilities I have achieved. You won't have to stumble through all the mistakes I made, but simply follow the correct path, and you will experience what I have experienced, and you will have sufficient time (50+ years) to discover where such abilities will lead.

A SPECIAL NOTE

For more information on Nine Square Diagram Boxing, including a larger and more advanced course, go to MonsterMartialArts.com, or to…

https://9squarediagramboxing.wordpress.com

AFTERWORD

There you go. Over 50 years of research and study, dozens of arts, pure workability in an easy to study format. There is only one problem.

In my career I have met maybe a dozen people who began the martial arts early in life, and never quit. The rest, 99.9%, Never began, or began and quit, or somehow dropped the ball on their dreams.

The hardest thing about the martial arts is to keep going. Deal with a wife and kids and career and whatever else you encounter. Nobody is saying not to. But to put aside your dreams just because somebody nagged you, or 'responsibility' called, or you need to make a few bucks and a few bucks and a few bucks…not good.

So let me tell you the secret. Something I realized early on, but that nobody seems to know, or at least to acknowledge.

This time, between birth and death is yours. It is yours to experience, to create, to do what you want. It is NOT somebody else's.

Do you know what it feels like, at the wrong end of 50 years of hard study and work? It feels good. Everybody my age is on walkers, or carrying oxygen tanks, or getting knee and hip replacements…and taking more pills than God has warts!

At 72 I have white hair but almost no lines on my face. Mentally I'm as sharp as I ever was. I freestyle with kids for hours, and watch them drop from exhaustion. I go out in a field and run like a kid…just because I enjoy life!

So, get to it. Start, or restart, the martial arts, no matter what your age. And don't quit.

Have a great work out!

Al Case

Appendix A
BELT RANKING

I usually teach the House forms from at the white belt stage. I usually teach sanchin and seisan at brown belt. But they do not have to be included in the system.

White belt (beginner)   roll back, ward off

Green Belt (intermediate)   punch under, snake/fair lady, crane

Brown Belt (advanced)   single whip, horn punch, rolling punch, slap grab

Black Belt (expert)   kenjutsu,

2nd Black Belt   monkey boxing

3rd Black Belt   instructor training

Fourth Black Belt (master)

Beyond this promotions are pretty much political. I have been recognized as a 9th degree Black Belt, but it is the 8th that was significant and important.

And, when I say active in the arts it means active. One doesn't quit for a couple of years and then come back and say he's been active. If you quit for a couple of years then you must not include that in your time spent training.

Appendix B

Following is a list of kicks I include in the system. I don't work on every kick every day, but rather work on maybe a variation of each of the four main kicks: front, side, wheel, crescent. The roundhouse and the wheel look similar, but the roundhouse impacts with the instep of the foot, and the wheel impacts with the ball of the foot.

Rear Foot kick ~ From the front stance kick with the rear foot and return.
> snap
> roundhouse
> side

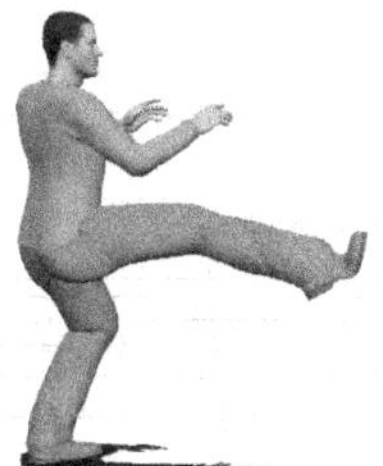

Front Foot Kick ~ From the horse stance kick with the front foot. Don't move the rear foot.
> side
> hook
> crescent

Front Foot Kick ~From the back stance kick with the front foot. Don't move the rear foot.
> snap
> roundhouse
> wheel

Skip Kick ~ From the back stance skip to the front foot and kick with the rear foot.

  snap
  heel thrust
  wheel

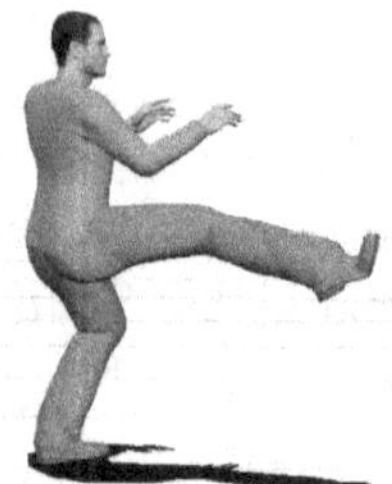

Skip Kick ~ From the back stance skip to land on the rear foot and kick with the front foot.

  snap
  heel thrust
  wheel

Replacement Kick ~ From a back stance replace the rear foot with the front foot and kick with the rear foot.

  snap
  wheel
  spin to rear side

Crossover Front Kick ~ From a horse stance cross over the front foot with the rear foot then kick with the front foot.

  snap
  roundhouse
  wheel

Crossover Rear Kick ~ From a horse stance step behind the front foot with the rear foot then kick with the front foot.
>   side
>   hook
>   reverse crescent

Secondary Kicks (kicks done immediately after first kick) ~ From the landing stance, step to the side (usually a triangle step) and kick.
>   snap
>   side
>   roundhouse
* do any kick, the side step and kick with other foot

Double Kicks Same Leg ~ From a stance kick twice with the same leg without putting foot to floor in between. It should go without aying that you must not not stagger or fall.
>   front wheel
>   front side
>   side roundhouse

Double Kicks Both Legs ~ Jump and kick with one foot then the other.

Obviously you can do a lot of mix and match with these kicks. They are all useful, practical, and based on the basics. So practice the basic-basics with them and really make them pop.

Unless you are kicking mid aid (not really recommended) you should always sink the weight at the same time as you land/kick.

MORE

For those students who wish to understand more concerning how Nine Square Diagram Boxing evolved was designed and put together, go to:

MonsterMartialArts.com

For explorations into the human soul through the martial philosophy of Neutronics, go to:

ChurchofMartialArts.com

And if you wish to simply explore my other writings,, including novels, poetry, etc., go to:

AlCaseBooks.com

On the following pages you will find a sampling of martial arts books.

introducing

Video Course Books!

MonsterMartialArts.com is publishing
a series of Video Course Books.
These are books which have links
to hours and hours of video.

No more mystery about what the teacher is saying.
No more wondering if you are doing everything right.
This is THE BEST teaching method in the world!

Go to MonsterMartialArts.com for more data…
MORE COURSES ARE COMING!

Books are no longer being distributed on Amazon.
Go to Draft2digital.com

ABOUT THE VIDEOS

Rarely, a link to a video won't work.

Try typing the link into your browser.
Try a different browser.
Try a different computer.

If no joy you can email me at aganzul@gmail.com.

www.ingramcontent.com/pod-product-compliance
Lightning Source LLC
Chambersburg PA
CBHW051126160726
47997CB00018B/483